The Rise and Fall
of the Hang Seng Index

JAKE VAN DER KAMP ('from the Commons'), is a native of the Netherlands, a citizen of Canada and a resident of Hong Kong for more than forty years. He has enjoyed a varied career, working first as an Asian investment analyst and then a financial columnist for Hong Kong's *South China Morning Post*. More recently he has turned novelist, rewriting old fairy tales told anew for today's times. In this book he returns to his career interests with a 'how to' manual on investment, which argues that you are already your own best adviser on when and what investments to make and should only rely on investment professionals for advice on how and where to do so.

Also by Jake van der Kamp

Non-fiction
Doctor! Doctor! An Investment Analyst on the Couch
Jake's View (columns from the *South China Morning Post*)

Fiction
The Emperor's Old Clothes
The Twelfth Fairy
Sinda Rella
The Seven Dwarfs
Eden Again

The Rise and Fall
of the Hang Seng Index

by

Jake van der Kamp

BLACKSMITH BOOKS

The Rise and Fall of the Hang Seng Index

ISBN 978-988-79639-1-2 (paperback)
© 2020 Jake van der Kamp

Published by Blacksmith Books
Unit 26, 19/F, Block B, Wah Lok Industrial Centre,
31–35 Shan Mei St, Fo Tan, Hong Kong
www.blacksmithbooks.com

Typeset in Adobe Garamond by Alan Sargent
Printed in Hong Kong

First printing 2020

Contents

INTRODUCTION: 9

CHAPTER 1: *The practitioners of the trade*   11

CHAPTER 2: *The tools of the trade*   75

CHAPTER 3: *Government and . . .*   115

CHAPTER 4: *Markets and the law*   145

CHAPTER 5: *The Asian markets*   171

CHAPTER 6: *Hot tips*   205

To a friend and colleague, Stephen Brown,
who may not agree with every thought expressed here
but will recognise a good number of his own.

INTRODUCTION

I am a retired investment analyst and financial journalist who has run across one too many blurbs for How-to-Beat-the-Market seminars and books. I hate to see people taken in by these things. The goddess Fortuna does not really favour those who devote themselves to her so completely. She has a way of rewarding casual worshippers more than she does ardent ones.

I say she has no rules written in stone for investment success and scorns her loud-mouthed, self-appointed priesthood. I say that very few people do consistently better than the market throughout their investment careers and these very few do so by virtue of their application, good judgement and patience, which are moral qualities, not learned tricks. I say that you are your own best investment analyst and that you abdicate your intelligence if you depend on others for investment choice. I say that you should treat the intermediaries of the market as just that, agents to carry out your investment decisions, not holders of original wisdom on investment value.

I am a Netherlander by birth and a Canadian by education and citizenship but my home is Hong Kong, one of the world's most bewitching cities. I have lived there for more than forty years, working first as an investment analyst covering Asian financial markets, and then as a journalist writing a daily column on Asian financial affairs for Hong Kong's *South China Morning Post*.

In this book I deal first with all the different types of investment adviser you are likely to meet and with why none of them can lead you to the promised land. I look also at the investment valuation tools that you are likely to use and why they are all blunt to varying degrees or will break in your hand. I then examine how and why government invariably gets it wrong when it dabbles in economic affairs and how bureaucratic empire-building makes the law see criminals where there is no crime. Finally, I review the different Asian markets which I covered over my career, country by country, and offer my opinions on what I think of the longer-term prospects of each.

Topping it off comes the 'ten hot tips' section required of any book on investment. Wanna make some money, folks? Well, you're in luck. Come on up and have your cash in hand. Jake's the name and stock's the game.

CHAPTER I

The practitioners of the trade

Mirror, mirror on the wall,
Who's the best stockpicker of them all?

Good question, even if it makes the answer obvious. Let's follow it right through anyway. Imagine yourself in a position that probably requires no imagination as you are probably already in that position. You have built up some savings and recognise that a bank savings account is no place to keep it. What little interest the bank may pay you on it is always less than the rate of inflation. You don't lose much but you always do lose.

There is obviously more out there, however, than just a bank savings account. There is a whole world of investment choices – stocks, bonds, currencies, real estate, commodities, gold – and every one of them can be held in different ways from plain vanilla ordinary shares to the fanciest derivative that any overpaid circus barker has ever put on offer. Take your choice.

Difficult, isn't it? It's like shopping for jeans and finding a hundred different variants on offer. Just ask, everyone tells me. So I ask for ordinary, plain, everyday jeans and the shop assistant looks at me as if I were something that crawled into the shop from the Cambrian period.

Well, okay, I'm in my sixties and that's how she looks at me when I ask. I have learned over time that what I want is not available in the kind of shop that sells a hundred different styles. I have to go to the sort of place that sells work boots and construction overalls.

My point is that a man whose children won't allow him out the door without running an inspection over him can still roughly find his way around a clothes shop. But he is also a man who is supposed to know his way around the investment business. It is the one he has been involved in for all of his working life. Yet I freely confess that I cannot tell you what to buy in the investment shop. What is more, I think no-one can reliably do it. Bearing that in mind, let's run down a list of those who hold out that they can.

The personal investment adviser
Financial consultant, retirement planner, securities counsellor; they go by any number of job titles. My advice to you when one has his hook dangling in front of your nose is that you schedule that first meeting with him for late on a Friday afternoon. This will allow you to pose your most important question immediately. It is one you pose to yourself, by the way, not to the investment adviser. Here it is:

If this fellow is so knowledgeable about where I should invest my money in ways to make it grow into a much bigger pile, why, on a gloriously sunny Friday afternoon, is he still sitting behind a desk in a rented office when he would much rather be out on his sailboat for the weekend or lifting a cold beer at a beach resort somewhere? Why is he still pitching strangers for his living instead of having left this office years ago for a life of ease funded by his investment winnings? If he really is so smart, why ain't he rich?

Yeah, very funny, hah-hah, now get real, you say. I am meeting this investment adviser because I know nothing about investment and he does know and I want to ask an expert in the field a few questions about where I should invest my money. What has this got to do with whether he is rich or not?

Put your brain back into gear. It has everything to do with it so let me just make the point again. If he really does know what investments will make you wealthier, why has he not long ago laid his hands on all the money he can find to make himself so wealthy through these same investments that he does not need to spend his time making a sales pitch to people like you? It truly is the first question you should ask yourself when meeting an investment adviser.

And the question has a straightforward answer. He does not know. He knows no more of what the future holds for your investment fortunes than does Madam Isadora with her tarot cards or the horoscope column of your newspaper. The only circumstances in which he could really be on to a guaranteed winner are also guaranteed to get him into deep trouble with his regulators if they were to find out. He would never share this winner with you anyway. It would be reserved for his personal account.

Any stockbroker can explain the problem to you. Ask him why the price has gone up and he will tell you that there were more buyers than sellers. Ask him why the price has gone down and he will tell you that there were more sellers than buyers. Ask him what the price will do tomorrow and he will also be glad to tell you, if you tell him first whether there will be more buyers or more sellers.

Now try to answer this question for supply and demand in the exchange rate of the US dollar against the euro. We are talking of tens of millions of people who take an active interest in this market, who regularly inspect the tea leaves of pronouncements made by the European Central Bank and the US Federal Reserve board, who follow all the official statistical releases or bore themselves daily with the pomposities of the *Financial Times*. And still they don't know. This is what you call an efficient market. It is very liquid, meaning that any trade in almost any size can be transacted in a split second. All the significant influences on it are a matter of public record and it reacts instantly to them. Knowledge of how the US$/euro exchange rate moves will help you explain how it moved in the past but will not tell you which way it will move in the future. By the time you can make a reasonable guess of where it is going, it will already be there.

On the other side of the investment business you have the very illiquid penny stock that moves only on the dictates of its controlling shareholders, or the market that is really no market because supply, demand and price are all rigged by the authorities (hello, Beijing). They are still efficient in that their prices still reflect the influences on them. The trouble is that the normal influences are restricted on the demand side and determined secretly or without reference to demand on the supply side. The benefit of investment is reserved in such markets for a favoured few – and here is a secret for you. You are not one of these favoured few. Nor is your investment adviser.

The quest for insight into the future is no more rewarding in the great bulk of the investment market between these two extremes. As a rule, by the time you have it figured out, the price has moved and your opportunity no longer looks as good as it did before.

Take note that I do not make this a hard-and-fast rule for all occasions. The market is chaotic. There are indeed some people who mostly win for long stretches of time. It is the way chaotic systems work. But no-one is always a winner and no-one is guaranteed to be one on any given occasion.

But back to that first meeting with your investment adviser where you will soon hear him resort to investment jargon. He will speak of such things as a 'total solutions package' and an 'investment strategy tailored to your needs'. It is impolite to yawn when he does this but you are excused nonetheless. The total solutions package you are looking for is an investment that rises in value, preferably while giving you a steady stream of investment income. Everyone wants that same total solution. There is no puzzle here that needs a solutions package.

Similarly, the investment strategy tailored to your needs means that your adviser will put a piece of paper in front of you, outlining five or more 'risk profiles' from low risk to high risk, all preceded by tick boxes. The descriptions of the different profiles do not tell you much except that the higher the expected investment return the greater the supposed risk. This is true in general theory but often is not true in practice. Investment is too dynamic and too chaotic to allow a consistent definition of risk profiles.

What matters, however, is that you tick one of the boxes and sign the paper, so that your adviser can file it. The regulator who oversees him requires this paper as a condition of his having any business relationship with you. If you do not sign the paper, he is permitted to show you only a bank savings account. He is more likely to show you the door then.

It all has the effect, of course, of making you think that he knows what he's on about. So you tick the medium-risk box (you know one eyebrow will go up if you tick the minimum risk box) and you ask him what rate of return you can expect for this level of risk.

The answer you will get, if he cannot avoid giving you one and he will certainly try dodging the question, is his guess of the lowest figure that you might be willing to accept and still appoint him to manage your portfolio. It is probably still a higher figure than he thinks he can consistently attain but this is his best way of getting and keeping the business. He has talked to people like you before. He can make a pretty good guess of what you are thinking. Take note, however, that all this thought, his and yours, has only to do with his psychology and yours. It has nothing to do with the actual value of any investment you make. This value, or at least as much as can be known about it, is already expressed by its price in the market, and includes the risk that what people may expect of it will not actually materialise. No single human can hold all these different considerations in mind and balance them properly.

Only a large number of people, each having a tiny share of the answer to the puzzle and each having an influence proportional to the resources at his or her disposal and the risk he or she is willing to take, can hope to do this. Even then, many of them, sometimes most, get it wrong. It is the way a market works. One single person can guess but in an efficient market no single person can *know*. You lay down your money and you take your chances.

So if your investment adviser ain't really that smart, what makes him an investment expert?

Simple. His expertise lies not in what investment is the best for you or when to make that investment but rather in how to do it and where. He must know from whom to buy your investment, how to make the transaction at the best price and lowest possible dealing cost, where to register and hold in custody the ownership of the investment, how to report it to you in compliance with all the applicable laws and how to arrange payment to the satisfaction of all concerned. If you should then choose to sell this investment again, he must know how to do all this in reverse.

I can safely assume that you yourself do not know how to do all this and thus you do indeed need to consult an expert in these matters to do it for you. You may eventually, of course, choose to do some of this over your smartphone without anyone else's assistance but you will still first need someone to set it all up for you, which requires definite skills. You will also be limited on your smartphone to the biggest and most liquid markets unless you are in a real hurry to lose money.

It is not a much greater task, however, than any bank teller can handle for you. Why then should your investment adviser be paid any more than the teller?

Back we go to where we started. It is because you are fool enough to think that your investment adviser can indeed see into the future and make you a wealthier individual. You are therefore paying him for fooling you. More fool you.

And you can be made an even greater fool. Leave alone that the fees your investment adviser charges you for his services are often unwarrantably steep, he has hidden ways of adding to them. As just one example, he will routinely tell you to put your money in a managed fund rather than buy individual stocks or bonds directly. This is not in itself a bad idea. My own portfolio holds a mixture of funds and direct investments in securities. You may do best in your first investment forays to buy only such funds. What your adviser will not tell you, however, except in a roundabout fashion far down the long disclaimer statement, is that he is paid a finder's fee by the fund for steering your money there. If you find out, his excuse will be that this rebate came from the fund, not from you.

From whom does the fund make its money? Do you really think it was not you who paid in the end? More fool you again.

What your adviser also does not tell you is that, over and above the fees you pay him, you now pay additional fees to the manager of the fund. Why two levels of fees (and with funds of funds three levels of fees) for what is really only one level of service? Why not cut out the adviser then and put your money directly with the fund manager? Good thinking. Less fool you. Your adviser will now pull his welcome mat from his door if you show up again.

What we are talking about here for the most part, however, is you at the start of an investment experience, with a smaller sum of money to invest. Let's go on a few years and assume you have enjoyed a successful career with a few windfall additions to your wealth, taking it up to another two zeros to the left of the decimal. We now come to a different class of investment adviser.

The private banker
It is mostly just a fancy name for investment adviser, of course, but there are some distinctions. For one, you need

no longer concern yourself quite so much with fees. Assuming you have not left your portfolio entirely to his discretion (best not), his fees will be a good deal less in percentage terms than the fees you paid as a smaller investor. His work load has not grown in proportion to the amount of money he manages for you.

Additionally, it should not trouble you as much that you are occasionally paying two levels of fees. Your portfolio will be more diverse than before and hold other funds as a matter of course. You do not want to trouble yourself with quarterly reports from them all, often in different currencies. You now get one quarterly report from your private banker, all set out in one currency and with proper accounting of investment income. It lifts a headache from you. That's why you pay him.

More to the point, although he works within a larger bank, he is likely to have a greater degree of independence from the other operations of his ultimate employer. When the lower level sort of investment adviser phones you with an enthusiastic recommendation, you always have to ask whether behind him is a slave driver cracking his whip over the dealing desk in an effort to rid the bank of an investment that it does not want to hold on its own books. A private banker will generally be seated on the other side of higher and thicker walls from this slave driver.

Best of all is a bank that does not have a commercial side but concentrates on investment management of personal wealth, a typical Swiss family-founded bank, for instance. I am well aware that these have historically had a name for conniving at tax evasion and helping the generalissimo keep his loot after he has fled the palace. But such practices are less prevalent among reputable private banks today. Morality aside, there is one obvious question you should pose yourself: What is more likely to bring down the value of your portfolio – the tax dodger, the generalissimo or having that portfolio lumbered with a duff investment that your bank's executives want to offload because it threatens their bonuses? I prefer investment advisers who limit their conflicts of interest with me.

But private bankers, like other investment advisers, cannot see the future. They stand on their dignity more, which helps to create the impression of wisdom, but their skills lie in how rather than where to invest. They also lean more to the purely conventional sort of advice that poses the least risk to their reputations.

I still kick myself, for instance, for not having the courage of my convictions to buy more of a Russia fund when it had fallen more than 80 per cent in value and my private banker called me to say I should sell my remaining holdings. His bank's research department had given up hope, he said. I told him that it was much too late to make that call, that I thought Russia no Argentina and that I was actually tempted to buy more. He dissuaded me. More fool me. The fund bounced straight back up, starting that same afternoon.

I don't really blame the bank. It had its reputation to protect. The Russia fund had become an embarrassment. To stick with it any longer might have given the bank a

name with its clients for not reviewing a bad call that it
knew had gone bad. This it could not afford, which I fully
understand. My point here is that private bankers are often
even more reluctant than lesser investment advisers to stray
far from the conventional opinion of the day.

This trait can have its uses. It is my belief that those who
consistently get a market wrong do so much more consistently than those who consistently get it right. Just search
for one of these valuable pundits and take the opposite
view. They really are worth finding.

But I concede two difficulties. The first is that people
who consistently get it wrong also tend to dither a great
deal and offer no firm opinions at all. The second is that
when they do make up their minds they are often so
applauded by their audiences for reflecting its opinion that
they are promoted and lost to you as contrary indicators.
If you are of a mind to look for them, however, they are
most commonly found offering their views in the house
publications of bank private client investment departments.

The guru
We now ascend to the top of the mountain where the
internationally known gurus sit and the world gathers
round to hear what has made them grow so rich. Most
purported investment gurus are actually more like comets,
blazing an ever brighter trail through the heavens on one
consistent call (usually 'Buy') that has proved right time
and again for their chosen markets. The difficulty is that

very few of these comets manage to round the sun and blaze their way back again. When it comes time to say 'Sell', they keep saying 'Buy' and then slowly sputter and go out. Let us, however, consider two gurus who have long shone bright.

Warren Buffett is a man who lives at 123 Anystreet, in any Anytown, USA, which I suppose is as good a description of Omaha, Nebraska, as anyone who has not been there can make. I passed through on the train once, recalled that the town had given its name to an invasion beach in France in 1944, and judged it not sufficient reason to stop.

Mr Buffett, I am told, drinks Coca-Cola and reclines in a La-Z-Boy chair. It is my guess that he also drives a General Motors sedan and grouses at having to mow the lawn. He is Mr Every American and understands his countrymen so well (he *is* his countrymen) that he has an instinctive feel for what goes and what does not in his country's stock market.

Put this together with a penchant for close reading of company accounts plus the great windfall of a thirty-year one-way support for stock markets in the interest-rate policies of the US Federal Reserve Board, and you have one of the world's most successful long-term records of investment.

My congratulations to all those who discovered Warren Buffett early and may I suggest to them that they encourage him to stay on his own patch in his investments. His international forays have not been equally successful. It's horses for courses in this business and his course is the United States.

As a good contrast to Buffett, consider the Hungarian-born George Soros, a man who knows from bitter experience how clumsily despotic governments can swing their weight and with what disregard for the happiness of their own people. He is good at spotting that sort of government. Malaysia was part of my patch when I watched him in the early 1990s train his sights on the Malaysian government, which had allowed its central bank to run off the rails and become one of the world's more fevered foreign-exchange speculators. This bunch took the view that British Prime Minister John Major was an honourable man and they ought to believe him when he promised that he would keep the pound sterling in the European Exchange Rate Mechanism, a precursor to the euro. They bet the house on him. George Soros' experience of government promises led him to take the opposite side of the Malaysian central bank's bet. He cleaned up in reportedly not too far short of a billion dollars when John Major cracked. They don't like George Soros in Kuala Lumpur.

But having scorned the US internet investment boom of the 1990s, Soros allowed his lead portfolio manager to change his mind and become its last big believer, just in time to skid out spectacularly when the internet boom collapsed in early 2000. It is horses for courses indeed in this business and for George Soros it means the world at large more than the United States.

This may seem to make Warren Buffett and George Soros complete opposites, but they shared one crucial element of support in their rise to fame. They were helped by the conceits of politicians and bureaucrats who rushed in where mere mortal financiers, leave alone angels, feared to tread.

In Warren Buffett's case this was the Federal Reserve Board depressing interest rates in order to stimulate the American economy. What the Fed actually did was stimulate a multi-decade bubble of financial speculation. Mr Buffett would have had a commendable record without it, but he starred because the entire US economy was used as an experimental test-bed for the novel economic theories of a handful of professors. In the case of George Soros, success was to a considerable extent the gift of regimes that were happy to waste immense fortunes on their own arrogance and ignorance. He suffered under them as a younger man. He benefitted from them as an older one.

The rule that no-one knows the future is not absolute. When markets are made inefficient by official authority it is sometimes possible, as Saint Paul put it, to see through a glass darkly. I admit it.

But you still have no guarantees. One guru I follow closely is David Stockman, who was President Ronald Reagan's budget director, a man of considerable experience and the author of several books well worth reading. He is a pessimist, largely because of Federal Reserve Board tinkering with the economy, and had long published a bear portfolio of investments around the world (mostly short positions) to save you money in the event of a crash.

This portfolio looked increasingly woeful as markets continued to go up and the loss positions grew greater.

Then Stockman took the portfolio off the bottom of his daily column in his Contra Corner website. It was almost the same day that the trend changed. I had reluctantly to rate him as one of those remarkable contrary indicator gurus. There ought to be a law. There isn't.

The fund manager
Here is a fact that professional fund managers do not like to share with you. Almost every study done on the subject shows that more than nine-tenths of the time they under-perform the market indices of the markets in which they invest. I say *almost* every study because if I say that *every* one of them shows it then someone will pop up to say it isn't always so in Nebraska and, yes indeed, Warren Buffett hails from Nebraska. But let me stick my neck out anyway. Every study shows it. The market always beats the professionals.

Let me define it a little further. In almost every financial market (the almost is honest here) there are indices that show you the average price movement of securities listed on that market. Some are all share (or bond) indices, the FTSE All-Share Index in Britain, for instance, and some, such as the Dow Jones Industrial Average, use a smaller representative sample. The sample is weighted by the rela-tive size of its members and this weighting is regularly adjusted by the people who administer the index to keep it honestly representative of the market. Compare the price movement of the stock you chose against the performance of the index over the same period and you have an indication of whether you have done better or worse than the overall market.

Except that these indices are not always as reliable as they are portrayed. Some of them, for instance, are not adjusted for dividend payments. This is no minor flaw. Take a $10 constituent of the index, which pays a 30-cent dividend. On the date that the dividend goes 'ex' (is paid and no further claims for dividends accepted) the share price will drop from $10 to $9.70 even if nothing else has changed. The shareholder has taken 30 cents out of the value of his holding and so loses nothing but the index says that he has lost that 30 cents. It is thus easy to outperform such an index. Just buy its constituents, hold them and the total returns value of your portfolio will outperform the index every year by the extent of the index dividend yield.

This is an example of a particularly egregious index flaw but there are many flaws or just plain inconsistencies between the different indices. Professional fund managers thus rely on indices that are calculated on a consistent basis across the world for their benefit. To match how fund managers organise their funds these indices come in a range of distinctions such as statement in local currency or us-dollar equivalent, in total market or only the proportion available to foreign investors, and in groups of markets such as 'Asia' or 'Asia ex-Japan'. There are two major providers of such indices: msci (Morgan Stanley Capital International), because what a win it is for Morgan Stanley to remind clients of who is the authority on markets, and the *FT*

(*Financial Times*), because a pompous financial newspaper also needs to burnish its status.

The thing about these indices, however, is that you, an ordinary member of the investing public, only get snippets of what they say about markets. If you want it all you have to pay MSCI or FT. Professional fund managers all do so and therefore they know just how well they stand relative to the real market performance, which also makes them happy that you are not told all, because they almost all underperform. I say that on a consistent long-term basis all of them do so. Go away, Warren.

They have little tricks for hiding it from you, of course. If the comparison with Asia ex-Japan looks bad try the 'all Asia' or 'Asia ex-Japan free float'. Switch to FT indices if you cannot get what you want from MSCI. The most common dodge is to present clients a chart with two lines, both starting from the same point. The top line shows how well the fund has done, the bottom one shows the comparison index. The trick is to pick a starting point just before the fund happened to get lucky, usually just after it was formed and had only a few million dollars to invest. Start the chart from any other date and the relative performance might not look all that good. But if the fund manager's luck is in he can ride that one starting windfall for twenty years of pulling the wool over your eyes. Charts tell wondrous lies.

If you find this surprising I invite you to turn back to the first page of this book and start reading again. It is what I have been saying all along so far. Fund managers have no better a crystal ball than you do. Their expertise lies in how and where to invest, not when and in what to invest.

In addition to this hard fact of investment life, however, fund managers have further difficulties in trying to outperform a market. In the first place they have to charge you a management fee. Office space, staff, regulatory oversight (a growing burden) and all other administrative matters are a steady drain on performance. They also have to pay dealing costs. Every time they buy or sell something for the fund, out goes a dealing commission, a stock exchange charge, a custodian charge and probably a regulator's fee. If they tell you that they have done nothing to change the portfolio this quarter you will tell them that you can do nothing, too, but you don't charge yourself a fee for it. They have to look busy to keep up appearances. All of this assumes, moreover, that they deal honestly. It is not a fool-proof assumption.

So why bother with fund managers at all?

The biggest single reasons are that they offer you diversity and investment administration. Take that diversity first. You are not looking for a horse-race gamble in financial markets. Well, perhaps, you might be and financial markets certainly do not take by far as big an intermediary's bite out of you as your bookmaker does at the races. But if a horse race is what you want, then put this book down, pick a hot stock, put all your money on it and enjoy the wild ride.

I assume here that your ambitions are a little more conservative than this and that you recognise the risk of putting all your money into one, or even two or three stocks. Investment in a managed fund will give you the diversity you want even if you have only a small sum of money to invest. You are likely to find that particular diversity attractive to you for at least part of your portfolio even if you have larger sums to invest.

And then there are the administrative headaches of where to lodge the paperwork, how to collect dividends and how to handle share splits, bonus issues, bond redemptions and calls for more capital. Your stockbroker will do it for you if you choose but then he will charge high fees for it or be nagging you every two days to churn your account with him because this is otherwise the only way he is paid. Investment is about putting your money to work for you but if it is also going to make you work for hours every day then what have you really achieved? I think this degree of obsession with personal investment a pretty good indication of a boring individual. Let the fund manager do it for you.

What many of them do is implicitly acknowledge that they are not really smarter than the market. They recognise that they do best simply by buying the constituents of the index against which they are measured in the same proportion that the index holds them. It is a low-cost way of investing. No research is needed and little dealing cost incurred. Match the index this way, the reasoning goes, and you can consistently outperform nine tenths of your competitors.

The most common way it is now done is through what is called an Exchange Traded Fund. The idea behind an ETF is that you do not give your money directly to the fund manager to invest in your chosen fund. You rather buy or sell that fund through its listing on a stock market. The big attraction here is that this is the very lowest-cost way of index investing. Administration fees can be less than 0.2 per cent a year. Your portfolio is likely to include an ETF.

But beware of one little cheat. 'Synthetics' are funds that track indices not by holding the stocks listed in the indices but by high-stakes bets on the performance of these stocks. There are fancy mathematical names for this but the maths does not always mimic reality as well as claimed. Sometimes markets make perverse movements and in times of crisis the odds on the gambles can change so quickly and market liquidity can dry up so suddenly that no trading system can respond rapidly enough. The principle to bear in mind here is that the exits of the stadium are never wide enough for a stampede. When things go wrong the synthetics are the first to be crushed. Avoid synthetics.

A fund does not have to be an exact copy of its market index, however, in order to track that market. Buy the blue chips of the market in rough proportion to their weighting in the market and your tracking of the index is likely to have an error of no more than a few per cent, which is close enough for most investors who want this sort of thing. It is in fact what any large fund does and cannot avoid doing. It holds more of the big stocks and less of the small stocks because the bigger ones are easier to buy and, more importantly, easier to sell. No fund manager wants to be caught with a big holding of a small stock if he should ever want to be out of it quickly. Thus you cannot really be a big

investor in any market and find yourself far out of line with
the index unless, of course, you want to give your holdings
a certain slant, say 'green' stocks only or no weapons or
tobacco stocks. But then you will usually find that one of
the professional index providers also puts out an index for
just the twist you want and your fund's performance still
closely tracks this index.

And last, a thought about hedge funds – RIP. Yes indeed,
rest in peace. They were a fine idea but only the remnants
are with us any longer. They were always misnamed anyway. Their most obvious characteristic was not that they
hedged their investments, that is to say, insured them in
some way against contrary movements. They were mostly
more leveraged than hedged in practice. They actually
stood out more by their fee structure, which was that they
charged clients nothing if the value of the fund went down
but a proportion of the gain, usually 20 per cent, if the
value of the fund went up.

I was a director of a small Singapore-based hedge fund
for a number of years and thus had a front seat to watch
the hedge fund industry's demise. What killed it was first
of all the complete failure through fraud of a big New York
hedge fund operator, Bernie Madoff. He lost his clients an
estimated US$18 billion in the end and after that it was
pulling teeth to get anyone to put money with any but the
biggest names in the investment business. The accomplice
in this extinction of hedge funds was regulatory costs. They
went up exponentially post-Madoff. My own personal
experience of it was being harassed with regulator threats

of proceedings for felony because I had forgotten to file my new passport number within the required short period after renewing it.

Who needs the headache? Our hedge fund eventually closed down, one of thousands that did so. But I am still proud of having been associated with an effort that did some great things for Asian start-ups.

The economist

Down we go now through the ranks of the investment advisers to the sort who talk even more macro waffle than the gurus but never follow it up with specific investment recommendations. This mundane task has been assigned to the people who inhabit the lower foothills. Economists are there to give you the economic overview.

I think they are best compared to astronomers. It can be a wonder to learn how the Crab Nebula originated from a supernova flash almost a thousand years ago or how the pulsation rate of the star, Delta Cephei, was a crucial clue in the quest for the size of the universe. But what can you do with this knowledge other than take joy in it as telling you something about your own existence? There is no money to be made from knowing how far it is to the nearest star. Astronomy is an observational science.

Likewise economics. It can tell you many interesting things about the relationship between human resources and human initiative in the context of human society. It can tell that if you pinch that balloon called the economy here it will pop out there and that if you push it this way it will roll that way. You can learn that trade flows for any country must balance with opposing investment flows or force a change in international reserves and how all this is likely to affect foreign exchange rates.

But what can you actually do with this knowledge of how money works to make some money? The answer is that you can do more than astronomers do as there are more jobs in economics than there are in astronomy and they generally pay more. This is about as far as it really goes. Economics is also an observational science. It is certainly not a technology. Its lessons are far too general to specify ways of making money. The most it reveals is that everything is linked through cause and effect and interventions generally create distortions that make things worse. You have heard it before. The road to hell is paved with good intentions.

This won't do, however. If the magicians cannot give the king precise divinations, then what is the use of magicians? If all they can say is 'Do good things and good things will result' then off with their heads. It is the constant dilemma that economists face and they resolve it by telling their political masters that they can indeed work wonders with the incantations they have learned in the university classroom.

They have mostly done it by conferring godlike status on one of their number from the early twentieth century, John Maynard Keynes, whose works are often unintelligible for their rambling and contradictory nature, which is all to the good because Keynes is dead and his works can then be made to say anything you want. The basic message is that by spending money government can stimulate economic activity and it is its responsibility to do this in order to create full employment.

Leave alone for the moment whether it is true that governments can actually do this. I think it false, which renders moot the question of whether they ought even to try to do it. I shall have more to say of this later. But my point here is rather that these ideas, loosely grouped under the heading 'Keynesianism', have a substantial public following, which gives economists employment as now they have authority to give advice to politicians. Along the way they can also tell investors how the things that politicians may do with this advice will affect the performance of the economy. Hotels in the central business district can thus make a lot of money by regularly filling their function rooms with lunch events hosted by banks to showcase the presentations of in-house economists.

Pity the poor clients who find themselves there. The salad may not be wilted and the rubber chicken not entirely rubbery but then they must sit through forty-five minutes of Keynesian blather of which they understand barely a word, all the while resolved not to display their ignorance if others seem to be paying rapt attention.

The fault is not theirs. The trouble, as the noted monetary economist Milton Friedman once said, is that many of his colleagues could say the words but could not sing the tune. How true. I once discovered from the writings of a Bank of England governor that he had little understanding of how the international balance of payments works, and he was a professor of economics. Such are the results of building an intellectual discipline on a foundation of shifting sands rather than on hard rock. Hard rock, however, allows for little more than an observational science and thus most economists opt for shifting sands. It means they talk a lot of waffle.

You can make the test yourself. How often have you heard or read an economist explain the interplay of supply, demand and price in the local taxi trade in your town? Where ride apps have not forced a change you will usually find enormous values assigned to taxi licences because the local authorities have tightly limited their issuance while at the same time having mandated a high level of taxi fares. It is an ideal subject for economic analysis and it could make a difference to you if you have ever considered investing in taxi licences.

But, no, the economists are all out making pronouncements about whether the us Federal Reserve Board, a classic collection of the king's magicians if ever there was one, will raise its federal funds rate by a quarter per cent next month. Great significance is imputed to this question and a storm of talk on the matter blows continually out of academia. You, however, will find that the market has already long factored in the prevailing odds on whether it will happen. There is no investment value left in the Fed talk. Best use the time more enjoyably and talk football instead.

The investment analyst

Now, let's go to one who really should know, whose written work is shovelled into your hands by every class of adviser: the investment analyst. This pundit spends his day hunched over his keyboard, scouring company reports, stock exchange announcements and obscure newsfeeds. He then performs arcane tasks with spreadsheet programmes to distil out of them the elixir of 'true value' and tells you of his findings via reports published under his bank's name.

Should you ever meet him, and chances are that you will not do so except in the company of a sales desk chaperone, two things will strike you about him. First, he is rather young to be an expert of this magnitude. They crowd a lot of information into kids' minds at university these days but, still, you know. . . .

The second thing you will notice is that he is a nerd. His clothes are mismatched, there are breakfast stains on his shirt front, and his eagerness to explain the minutiae of his trade seems more suited to a rocketry lab.

I am talking here about the real investment analyst, not the one labelled so in your video feeds. The latter does not trouble himself much with number crunching and rarely reads financial statements, even assuming he understands them, which quite often he does not. His strengths lie in being articulate on air with a calm, assuring voice, and an ability to worm his way around uncomfortable questions. This analyst spends his time in the front office on the phone with clients, not around the back, looking at investment ratios.

I nonetheless mostly prefer him to the nerd. Aside from the fact that he is invariably much better company, he is more likely to have his finger on the pulse of the market, although I have to admit that this does not give you much. The pulse reading is rarely good for more than a few hours. Yet the nerd can rarely give you any diagnosis at all. Price is a mystery to him. He can tell you whether a company has decent prospects for growth or is financially troubled and there it stops.

Yes, he knows he should be able to do more. He knows he has been hired to tell you whether to buy or sell the stock. But he has also learned from his bruises that if he recommends the good prospect his sales people will say, 'Come on, have you seen the price recently? Gone up like a moon shot. Why didn't you tell us last month?' And if he tells them to sell the financially troubled stock they will say, 'Too late again. I can't tell my clients to sell anything that has already fallen like a rock. And thank you ever so much, by the way, for telling us to buy it last year.'

So he does his best to avoid outright 'Buy' and 'Sell' recommendations, particularly 'Sell'. I once had an object lesson in the dangerous implications of this word as a nerd in the investment research department of a stockbroking company. The market was dropping badly and the London sales office sent me a list of 100 stocks for which they wanted ratings: 'A' for sound, 'B' for troubled and 'C' for goner. I gave six companies a 'C' rating, our London sales people told their clients, these clients told other brokers, the other brokers told the 'C' companies. I came in to work next day hanging on to my job by my fingernails. Fortunately, my top boss was understanding about it all despite having business associations with some of these companies. I was to apologise to them for playing with fire, he said, but would not have to retract if I really thought they were in serious trouble.

I expect no kudos for the subsequent fact that all six soon went bust. Everyone knew they would do so. With one exception, everyone also knew that you only invited trouble by saying so in public. I learned my lesson. From then on, no more 'Buy', 'Hold' and 'Sell' recommendations. My vocabulary became: 'Buy', 'Buy on Weakness' and 'Long-Term Buy'. I have since seen even better euphemisms for 'Sell'. My favourites are 'Disaccumulate' and 'Source of Funds'.

You might think it odd that investment research should be such an agglomeration of nerds. It seems on the surface to be a centre of intellectual challenge, the place where investment ideas are conceived. And indeed it had this reputation at that same brokerage house in which I learned my lesson about 'Sell' recommendations. The families of the high-born pushed their children our way on graduation from university. Investment analysis is the starting gate in the race to commercial glory, they believed. My immediate boss on the sales desk recognised this thinking and warmly welcomed the new trainees of this class when they showed up, invariably on a Monday morning.

'But before we get started, you'll want to come up to speed with the others here,' he would say. 'Just sit at that desk now and I'll bring you what you need.'

He would then go to our research library and tell the librarian, 'Shirley, let's have "S" and "T" today.'

Shirley would thereupon pull out a selection of file folders on companies with names beginning with the letters 'S' and 'T' and our man would heave them onto the desk of the new trainee – 'I would like you to brief yourself on these.'

This unfortunate soul would then be left entirely on his or her own for the week. Few lasted it out. But if they were still in place by Friday afternoon they could keep their desks. The ordeal was a way of filtering out recruits afflicted by attention deficit disorder, a frequent condition of the children of the high-born. The polar opposite, obsession, a characteristic of nerds, is more to be valued in research.

My boss had other filters as well. He valued good additions to his sales desk more than he did to research and research was one of his hunting grounds. Any woman there who had the nerve to contradict him, but politely, in front of others, or make some mild remark at his expense to his face and then laugh, was a candidate. For men he had a different test.

'Come and join me and the lads at the Bull and Bear this evening,' he would say, and the fellow would then be stood at the bar and urged to keep up speed with the others through four quick pints of beer. If he was still standing at the end and capable of coherent speech he might expect an invitation to the sales desk. He had clearly had training in sociability, a valuable trait in sales.

The end result in every case was that the nerds stayed in research and those more socially adept used it as the first rung of the ladder to success in stockbroking. That's how investment research gets its nerdish taint.

Few of the nerds have much time in reality to delve deeply into the affairs of the companies they follow. They are always under pressure to guess the next quarterly earnings numbers for every company they cover, to write a report about their guesses, message the major clients about it and write another report when the earnings numbers are actually announced. Few bother to read the detailed annual corporate accounts. They have already done their pre- and post-earnings reports by the time these are published. The most notice they will take is to plug a few bits into their automatically (mindlessly) updated spreadsheets.

The best way to get a prediction roughly right is, of course, to cheat a little. This is best done by applying one's energies to finding out what other analysts covering the stock are guessing. Put your own guess right in the middle and your job is safe.

A bigger cheat is to ask the companies themselves, which analysts are not supposed to do but which was the practice of the most successful bank analyst I ever met. He never asked directly, of course. He knew how to phrase his questions and how to guide the answers. But the senior bankers he met were mostly happy to accommodate him if all was spoken in code. They knew him well enough to know he would never rat on them and it served their purposes to keep the market correctly apprised of the trend of their earnings. They could also do it as the rules required, of course, and send a notice to the stock exchange but this route was best reserved for major earnings surprises.

And yet all this attention to quarterly earnings numbers is largely a waste of time and effort. Share prices rarely make their big moves on these numbers. The market already knows, not through insider gossip but through the fact that the market for any reasonably traded investment is made up of millions of people all making their own small guesses in their own small ways to the extent of the wealth at their disposal and the risks they are willing to take. At the micro level of your personal choice all is chaos and uncertainty. Only at the macro level summing millions of people making their choices, a result to which you contribute but which is unfortunately invisible to you except in hindsight, can the future be revealed. The village decision is rarely wrong. Too bad you asked the village idiot.

The technical analyst
And now let's have the village witchdoctor. Listen to any audio feed on the market and you will soon hear mention of 'moving averages', 'resistance points' and 'support levels'. You are in the presence of a modern-day augur who sees the future by reading the entrails of the market.

Okay, that's not entirely fair. I accept that investment trends are made by humans and where you have many people taking an active interest in an investment you have the play of mass psychology. Take the daily opening, high, low and closing price of any stock or market index over a number of years, plus the daily volume of trading, and it should be possible in the resulting chart to see patterns that reveal this mass psychology.

I can tell you of one such pattern immediately. It is probably the oldest ever noticed and, while you cannot guarantee its reliability for investment decisions, it shows up much more often than coincidence would dictate. It is called a 'head and shoulders reversal formation'. Take a share price that has gone far up and then retreats to lose some of its gain. This is the first shoulder. Next, the price goes even further up, above the first shoulder and retreats once more. This is the head. Finally the price goes up one last time, although not as high as the head, and then collapses. This is the second shoulder. Check throughout for volume confirmation. The heaviest volume of trading should be throughout the first shoulder, less through the head, and less again through the second shoulder. Now draw a straight line from the bottom of the retreat from the first shoulder through the bottom of the retreat from the head and keep that line going. If that final retreat from the second shoulder goes through this line, says the chartist, then sell all you have. This thing ain't coming back for a long, long time, if ever.

It is my guess that one can draw the same chart for famous battles of history. Take, for instance, the Battle of Stalingrad, the turning point of the Second World War.

After a long advance against growing Russian resistance, the German army tires and pulls back a little. Then it rallies, pushes forward again even further but is again halted and forced back. Finally it makes one last try and gains a little ground although less than in its previous push. But by now it is exhausted and is sent reeling back, never to return again. If it were possible to observe in hindsight, I think you would also find the first assault the most savage, the second less so and the third less again. Make this the French versus the British 127 years earlier and you have an approximation of what happened at the Battle of Waterloo. I shall let the psychologists have their say here but I think it reflects the way the human mind in mass psychology works in reversals of fortune.

The trouble is that you do not often see a head and shoulders and you cannot by sure it really is one when you think you see it forming. Sometimes the second shoulder goes higher than the head, sometimes there is no volume confirmation and sometimes the chart is just a straight scramble of noise. Even when you are sure you have one and you call others you are easily told, 'Too late. I can't get out now anymore.' And then you have the times it all proves false. The head and shoulders speaks truth more often than not but occasionally it does not. You can just never be sure.

And that's not good enough for the witchdoctor. He is asked on a daily basis what the entrails show and he must have a response. He is a commentator whose following quickly vanishes if he says, 'Hold' too often.

If nothing else will do he can always resort to moving averages. The chart shows that the track of the share price has crossed upwards through its 50-day moving average. That's a Buy signal. Oh, it hasn't crossed yet? Let's make it a 30-day moving average then and we'll have a cross. A good meta rule is, the more lines that the technical analyst draws on the chart the less certain he is of what it means.

I remember our technical analyst at one shop where I worked showing an American client a chart he had entirely filled with squiggles and arrows.

'Do you understand?' he asked.

'Oh, perfectly,' said the client. 'I have only one question. Who was the running back on that last play?'

The sales desk generally likes technical analysis or at least its simulation. Listen to the client chatter on the desk in the morning and a sizeable proportion of it is about resistance, support, break-out and the like. My own view is that I have time for technical analysis but the clock is running on it.

I should also tell you that the technical analyst is often as much of a nerd as his colleague, the investment analyst. You will mostly get his thoughts at second hand and you will not find them as frequently or prominently published as the investment analyst's. Head office has reservations about the witchdoctoring business.

The bond analyst

Most of what I have been talking about so far deals with the stock market. But you are also likely to consider bonds for your portfolio. With bonds you don't share in the upside if the share price takes off. You only get your regular coupon (interest) payment and repayment of the principal when the term of the bond is up. Bondholders, however, are paid out before shareholders when a company fails. A holding of bonds thus gives your portfolio a greater element of stability and security.

This, at least, is the majority view. You may occasionally see evidence to the contrary, for instance in nineteenth-century American railway bonds sold to European investors. Not worth the paper they were printed on, people say, but it is not quite true. Framed and hung up in the boardroom they are worth a great deal as a stark reminder of investment folly. If you wish to say it is a lesson fully learned in times past and not needed again today, I shall ask you whether the spelling of Argentina has changed since times past.

Nonetheless, your investment adviser is likely to suggest that you consider bonds, either directly or, most likely, through an investment in a bond fund. If you have enough money to be dealing with a private banker, you will be convinced to do so through homilies about the unwisdom of putting all your eggs in an equities basket.

What then makes the bond analyst different from the equities analyst? In outline very little. They both have the same job of analysing a company's financial position and they use mostly the same tools to do it. The first is meant to determine whether a company's financial circumstances justify the present bond price while the second ponders whether they justify the present share price. In both cases the task is beyond them. The prices of both equities and bonds are determined by the company's financial circumstances. What nonsense then to ask whether the financial circumstances justify the price. My pardons. Have I said this before? I may do so again.

The assumption on which both analysts must therefore work is that sometimes the market gets it wrong. This is a dangerous assumption to make as the record shows that it is mostly the analysts who get it wrong in such cases. The record also suggests that when bond analysts get it wrong they do so more spectacularly than their equities counterparts.

There is a reason for this. With a few exceptions, equities analysts are paid out of the commissions, fees and other squeezes charged to clients who buy investments from their related sales desks. Bond analysts, however, are paid from the fees charged to companies that they rate. Let me stress this critical distinction. The people who buy the bond do not pay for the rating. This fee is paid by the company whose bonds they buy. There are structural reasons that the bond market evolved this way but what it comes down to is that bond analysts have a big incentive to please the companies they cover and less incentive to please the bondholders.

It is especially so because most bond analysts do not work with bond sales desks, as equities analysts work with equities sales desks. Bond analysts rather work mostly for professional ratings agencies, in particular two giant ones operating across the world, Standard & Poor's and Moody's. Rarely will any sizeable new bond pass the muster of the overseers of any debt market unless one of these two has put out a ratings opinion of how reliable it thinks the issuer's promise to repay the debt. These ratings range all the way from top investment grade to absolute junk and the agency uses the same scale for every bond that it rates. This has never been possible with equities which is why equities analysis remains fragmented while bond analysis has been unified under the two ratings giants.

The unity comes at a cost. Every rating ought to carry a prominent declaration – Warning: Paid for by the ratee. None do carry this warning, except occasionally in buried small print.

The ratings agencies say, of course, that this is the only way they can operate and I believe it is true. I only wish they would be much louder in admitting it. But they also say they recognise their obligation to the investing public to render honest opinions and are not unduly influenced to favour the companies they rate.

I say it is not so. The client is the one who pays and the agency has an incentive to please this client. A conflict of interest then exists with bondholders who are given to believe that the opinion is an independent one. The system invites dubious ratings.

But you don't have to take just my word for it. Look up the history of ratings in the United States alone and you will find howlers aplenty in debt instruments rated sound only shortly before their failure. It was particularly notable during the 2007–08 financial crisis. Because of these problems, in the 1990s a new way of rating bonds evolved: the credit default swap (CDS), essentially a form of insurance against bond default. If you hold a CDS on a bond you owe the issuer of that CDS a regular payment until the bond matures. If all goes well and the bond holders are fully paid out then you, the holder of the CDS, get nothing. If, however, the bond defaults, the issuer of the CDS owes you the outstanding principal of the bond holdings the CDS covers and all the outstanding interest payments. These CDS instruments are traded on the market and their price at any given time is an indication of how sound the market thinks the underlying bond.

Let me repeat my mantra. I am a great believer in the superiority of overall market opinion to the opinions of individuals who think they know better than the market. I think the market pricing of a CDS is incomparably better than the opinions of the analysts employed by ratings agencies as a measure of the soundness of debt.

But the CDS has not yet knocked the ratings agencies out of the way. In the 2007–08 financial crisis the CDS was held in part to blame for sparking off the crisis, which indeed it did do. If it had not, the crisis would have come later and been much worse. The CDS was the market's first messenger on the coming debacle and people blamed the messenger.

There are admittedly some difficulties with using a CDS as a substitute for a formal rating. I have given a simple explanation of how a CDS works but it is not an entirely simple instrument and a number of derivative forms have evolved, each with their own special quirks, which makes it difficult to rank creditworthiness. In addition, CDS contracts are not traded on any formal exchange, they are not subject to any formal reporting requirements and they are not secured. If you hold a CDS and your counter-party cannot pay, you lose. The price of a CDS therefore may reflect this counterparty risk as well as the risk of the underlying bond. In short, this superb rating tool is still one for the professionals. May it graduate to general public use soon.

Thus to my advice on bonds. More than for their equities equivalents, I think you do best to buy bond funds rather than individual bonds. The market is generally efficient, often more so than in equities, but often also less liquid. A company will have only one class of ordinary shares but may have issued many bonds, all of different maturities and coupons. Let the bond fund managers sort all this out.

Most of all, bear in mind that the opinions of bond analysts are heavily compromised.

The real-estate analyst

Here is a creature that does not exist, which may seem strange when you consider that your home is likely to be the biggest investment you will ever carry. Surely there must be independent advice available for an investment so important to so many people.

I do not say there are no such advisers. I only say they are not independent. More than in stocks and bonds, more than in any other field of investment, the people who bill themselves as analysts in the real-estate trade are sales representatives, not researchers.

There are good reasons for this. In real estate there is no absolute commonality of investment. One unit of a bond is exactly the same as any other unit of that bond and one share in the common stock of a company is exactly the same as any other share. But apartment 4C of a residential building is not exactly the same as 5C although they may be the same size and have the same layout. 5C is one floor higher and may have a better view or be less subject to traffic noise and therefore worth a slightly higher price or rent.

Take note that here we have considered only identical units in a single building, while not even beginning to look at pricing differences within and between the districts of a single city. These can be vast, taking in such factors as commuting times, amenities, incidence of crime, relative wealth of the inhabitants and even ethnic make-up, which is not meant to make a difference in a modern inclusive society but obviously still does.

Then we have differences between cities, which can also be vast, taking in different regulatory, bylaw and planning environments. Finally, we have the differences at the national level where we must add perspectives of currency, immigration law and political foibles such as that capital cities always get a disproportionate share of the national budget for cultural amenities. Meanwhile a share of Apple Inc. is the same thing in a Naples slum as it is in a high-rent district of San Francisco.

Professional research and advice in real estate therefore tends to be general, covering at its most detailed only district and sometimes only city. This does not help you much if flat 5c happens to be on the market and you want to put in a bid. Then you get only its estate agent. You are on her ground and she reads you better than you read her. All her advice is geared to closing that deal and taking a deposit, if not for 5c then for something like it and the sooner the better. Can you trust her?

Yes, you generally can. You should not really find it objectionable that she has her fangs out for the sale. You want it, too, or you would not be talking to her. Nor can she squeeze you for more than the apartment is really worth. No-one knows what it is really worth. There is in fact no such thing as 'really worth' here. The market price is what you and the seller agree, no more. The higher your bid the more likely that the sale will go through, which will please the agent. But still she can only tell you in what range of price your bid has a chance of being accepted. Do not ask her to tell you more and do not fault her if you later think you paid too much. You have a case against her only if the seller is in some way related to her and she benefits directly from the sale but did not tell you so.

You have to trust her anyway. You have no choice. You enter this market perhaps only once in your entire life and, however big the transaction is for you, the career specialists in the market will not go far out of their way for a one-transaction client. They will certainly not gear whatever research they may do on the market to the exact pricing circumstances of apartment 5c . You are going to find yourself where all other first-home purchasers find themselves when they come to this decision, which is gnawing their fingernails, unable to sleep well and hating the tension. Take consolation that it doesn't last.

Things are different, of course, if you have added a few zeros to your net worth and are looking at real estate not as your own home but as pure investment in which you hope to see your net worth grow even further. It is a common choice. Many people prefer real estate to the stock and bond markets. At a certain point of wealth you will almost certainly have investment property in your portfolio.

But here is the thing. Investment property is a nuisance to manage. You can leave shares and bonds with a formal custodian whom your investment adviser can find for you and who will do a competent job of collecting dividends and handling such things as share splits. What do you do, however, when your tenant phones late in the evening to tell you that the toilet inlet pipe is leaking and will you please come around to fix it? What do you do when the owners' corporation tells you that 5c is behind on contributions to the sinking fund for repair of external plumbing and you never even knew this fund existed? It's just headache and niggling little costs at every turn. Yes, you can appoint an agent but if you are just a one-unit client you will still have that agent tossing you most of the problems unless you pay the agent so much that there is very little left for you.

So here is one piece of advice on real estate and investment. Do it directly in a small way only if you are a handyman who likes pottering around with other people's plumbing and curtain rails. If this is not you, then consider such proxies as real-estate investment trusts and mortgage funds, which you can find on offer at your local bank branch.

The next step up is ownership of an entire block of apartments. At this level I think it begins to make real investment sense. Agents will find it commercially viable to take up your management headaches and you can also afford lawyers and accountants to deal with incorporation and tax problems. At a certain size of investment the cost of these professional services diminishes relative to your investment income and you can relax. You may even be lucky and link up with a management agent you trust, who offers to cut you in on a private ownership sharing arrangement he has set up. This may give you many of the benefits of a larger property investment at a lesser cost. Call it your good luck if it comes your way but don't think it your due.

Of course, when you buy the larger block you will still be fretting about how you can really know what it's worth and whether you are paying too much. You will have more detailed advice available but you will still have to chew those fingernails for a few days. No-one can give you an exact answer. The value is what you are willing to pay. That's the business of investment in real estate. Get used to it.

The gold bug

This class of investment adviser usually distinguishes itself by self-employment. Banks and other big financial concerns rarely sponsor ardent gold bugs. To find them, sign up for almost any private investment newsletter and you will see gold praised on every page, not analysed, not researched, just praised. We are talking old-time religion here.

The old-time message is always the same. Gold is the only sure measure, the final benchmark, of real value. The developed world made a mistake when it took its currencies off the gold standard and made them subject only to the self-discipline of central banks. When the apocalypse comes, however, gold will again take its rightful place as the only real store of value. Best prepare yourself for it now as the price of gold will rise long before the apocalypse is upon us.

It is not all nonsense. The self-discipline of central banks has certainly been a questionable substitute for the strict monetary discipline that the gold standard imposed through forced interest-rate movements. There is also no denying that gold roughly held its value against the everyday necessities of life for all of recorded history until about two centuries ago.

But therein lies the difficulty. Gold had been reliably steady for millennia because the amount of it available to commerce times its speed of turnover in commerce had been roughly equivalent to the gross domestic product (GDP) of the countries that relied on it for commerce. This made gold ideal as a backing for money. Fix your country's currency to gold at a definite price per ounce of gold, which automatically gave you a fixed exchange rate to all other currencies based on gold, and you had sound money. It was an immutable law of the cosmos.

By the late 1800s, however, economic growth was out-stripping the availability of gold across the world and the impact on the gold standard could not be avoided. In the same way that more growth in money than in production leads to inflation, less growth in money than in production leads to deflation. There were pronounced bouts of falling prices and these slowed the wheels of commerce. Things got so bad at one point that a US presidential candidate campaigned on the slogan, 'You shall not crucify mankind upon a cross of gold'. He wanted silver introduced along with gold as a backing for the US dollar. It did not happen. The gold standard wallowed along for another eighty years, popping its rivets at every turn, its 'fixed' purchase rates against the world's currencies increasingly being refixed, and then finally sank in 1971 when the US abandoned all US dollar links to gold.

What we have taking its place today, at best, is central banks targeting the growth rate of M2 (a measure of a country's total money supply) times their estimate of M2 volatility to equate exactly to GDP growth. If they could do it, and wanted to do it, the world might have an acceptable substitute for the gold standard. The influential American economist, Milton Friedman, who was instrumental in moving the world off the gold standard, thought they could do it. He was proved wrong. He has even been proved wrong in thinking they wanted to do it.

But there is no going back to the gold standard. Sorry, you gold bugs, but you cannot raise the dead and this one is dead. Breathing life into a corpse would be easier than redistributing gold across the world in correct proportion to national wealth, denominating all financial assets across the world in gold units at a fair exchange rates to present currencies and then reliably guaranteeing the availability of gold in exact proportion to world GDP growth. It cannot be done. Forget it. If you scorn present-day monetary arrangements then turn your attention instead to crypto-currencies and the possibilities of blockchain technology.

So what do we have in gold now?

Think of the properties that originally made gold so valued. It is lustrous, malleable, rare and a good conductor. The spoon in the coffee cup on my desk, however, is also lustrous, as shiny as I could want with its chromium steel alloy make-up. So is the wrapper of the chocolate bar I just unwrapped. So is the glossy Microsoft logo on my laptop. We live in a world of lustre now. Who cares?

Take the malleable. So is my coffee spoon if I put just a little muscle into bending it, so is the chocolate wrapper, endlessly so, and so even might that Microsoft logo be if I threw my laptop off the balcony because the software gremlins have wiped out my copy again. We don't even consider malleability today. If we need it, some cheap industrial process has done it for us.

As to rarity, let me just mention the spoon and the chocolate wrapper again. Lustre and malleability are costly qualities no longer. Lustre is not even desirable. We now associate it mostly with the flashy tastes of the nouveau riche. The only property of gold that has real value these days is its conductivity. This has uses in electronic and heat shielding applications. In short, the whole concept of a distinction between precious and base metals is now dated. They are all base metals now.

There is, however, more to take into account when considering gold as an investment. The formal distinction between an investment and a speculation is that an investment generates a return to the holder in the form of a regular profit or dividend. This can be measured, compared to other investments and made the basis of valuing the investment relative to others. With a speculation there is no return, only a belief, which may be based on sound reasoning and then again may not be, that the price will go up.

With gold there are no returns, no profit and no dividends. There are only costs in storing and providing security so that it is not stolen. Gold is a speculation, not an investment.

This does not say the price cannot go up. All I say is that the price of gold remains as high as it is because gold was for so many years the basis of the gold standard, and prized for its lustre, malleability and rarity. I very much doubt that its high conductivity alone could ever justify this price now.

And if I am right then the long-term future of the price of gold is down. I expect it to be a very gradual downtrend with lots of bounces back up. Something as deeply worked into the human psyche in so many cultures for so long a time does not quickly disappear. Slow as the current might be, however, you swim against it when you hold gold. Why bother?

But don't bother saying so to the gold bugs. For them gold is religion. You will get about as far as you do with street evangelists.

The art dealer

I once attended an art auction. It was on board a big cruise ship and the paintings, mostly of the genre commonly seen hanging on the walls of living room mock-ups in furniture stores, had been on display for days in the hallway leading to the main dining room. With each came a suggested price. On A-Day the auctioneer, fully equipped with a plummy English accent and artistically long hair, took his place behind a Sotheby's-style lectern, flanked by two gorgeous, aproned assistants, and proceeded to talk up his wares – 'If you like it, just raise your hand. We'll take care of everything. The next place you'll see it is in your home.'

And with that he was off, ably helped by a salting of cruise ship personnel in the audience to keep the enthusiasm (and the prices) up. I was astounded at what some of the sludge on offer then fetched. What a brilliant scam.

But not like a real art auction, you say.

Oh, yes it was, say I. In investment terms this was exactly like a real art auction, no different at all.

The difficulty with art as an investment is that, more even than gold, art is a speculation. Gold really does have everyday uses for which a value can be determined even if it returns no regular stream of earnings. All commodities are like that. Grain, copper, oranges and wool are all things important to human life. We can price the present demand for them, even our estimates of future demand, relative to supply and to possible alternatives. Doing it helps ensure a steady supply and all society benefits from this.

But who needs art? I am not trying to be a scoffing yokel here. I am only trying to put art into the context of investment and there is no context in which it fits there. The necessary link with price is entirely missing. The value of art can be measured only in aesthetic thrills and this is a unit of personal judgement alone. In money terms any piece of art is as little worth $1 as it is worth $1 million, whatever the price tag the art dealer puts on it. All he has to go on is that the last time an equivalent work by this particular artist was offered at auction it fetched $1 million. That the art market has any stability at all in money terms is only because art ownership is a very effective way for the super-rich to boast of their riches without giving the nearest taxman an opportunity to jump on their heads.

I am not saying it is worthless. I am only saying its place on a scale of worth denominated in money terms is purely arbitrary. Buy a work of art by all means if you fancy it but do not include it in your investment portfolio.

The journalist

And now we turn from the front-line trenches of the investment business to that immense army of commentators in the rear. Let's get down to the basic rule about journalists right away – It's in the price if it's in the press.

Just think about it. You check your morning newsfeed one morning and find that a pharmaceutical company in which you hold shares has been hit with a contamination scandal. Your first thought is that you should immediately sell these shares.

Stop. Don't do it yet. Here is the question you need to ask first. Why should you do it immediately?

Don't be stupid, you say. The point is to be out of this dog of a stock before the share price drops.

Very good reasoning, say I. But have you looked at that price yet? Do you really think you are the first person to have heard of this contamination scandal if you got the news from a public newsfeed? Do you really think that others who got the news did not have the same reaction you did and already put in their sell orders? And do you really think the share price has not already dropped in reaction to the news?

In fact, say I, take it from me that the initial reaction on bad news has momentum and often takes the price too far down at first. There are people who know the company, who will have a better idea than you do of just how damaging this news really is to the company's prospects, and they will jump in if they think the share price has overshot its mark on the way down. That could be you who gives them their bargains, just before the bounce back up. Best do nothing at all. There are some events that you just put under the general heading of Risk and take in your stride when they occur. You can no longer do anything about them. It's in the price if it's in the press.

I don't expect to be made welcome at the bar of the Foreign Correspondents' Club by saying all this but there are some things you should know about journalism and journalists. For starters, it's a trade, not a profession like medicine, law or accountancy. To enter a profession you must spend years in a classroom acquiring a defined and detailed knowledge and then more years as an apprentice. Your admission is subject to a regulatory body of your peers, which has the right to discipline or even expel you from the profession for misconduct. It also interacts on your behalf with official authorities in matters related to the profession.

Journalism has nothing like this. There is no specific body of knowledge to acquire, no recognised standards of admission, no official regulator of membership. You hold your job at the whim of your employer and call yourself a journalist because it says so on your calling card and because no old hand in the trade has yet told you that a journalist is defined as an unemployed reporter. Most of all, you are not well paid, particularly if working freelance. Journalism is a way-stop on the way to the poorhouse. Your stairway to higher things in journalism is the exit stairway.

The trade is not happy about all this of course and universities everywhere have taken advantage of the disgruntlement by setting up journalism schools at which the unwary can run up enormous personal debts over two or three years, learning about the ethics of journalism. I shall offer you my shortcut. Ethics lies east of Wethics and north of Suthics. If you have not learned moral behaviour at your mother's knee you won't find it at your J-prof's.

What you need for journalism is the classic liberal arts discipline of read, write and critique. And then do it again and again until you know what a cogent argument is and can compose one yourself. After this learn to type ten-fingered at sixty words a minute, still a useful skill, even in the audio-visual age, and learn the structure of your society. Who is the chief of police and what are his powers, who is the director of public works? Now go sit in the newsroom with a reporter and take a few knocks. I got mine when the city editor pushed my copy on the floor (this was still typewriter days) and turned away to put his head back in his hands. I picked up the several sheets of paper and took them to my mentor's desk – 'George, ahh ... listen ... could you...?' and was told, 'Now, young Jake, got between a man and his hangover, did you?'

Even in those days, journalism was something you fell into rather than chose. It doesn't really attract self-starters. Aside from the dedicated lefties who treat it as a calling and who do usually make the best reporters, it is for bright but lazy people. Yes, bright, I concede it. Don't forget the lazy.

This has big implications for financial journalism. I have nothing against sociology and English studies but they do not help you much in calculating a net present value. And yet this choice of studies is where most business journalists start out. For further experience they have rarely done more than cover politics at city hall. It helps them learn to make deadline but does not help them learn to read a balance sheet, which only a minority of them ever take the trouble to do.

Then again, if they really took an interest in corporate accounts or the valuation of investments, they would not long remain journalists. They would take the exit stairway when opportunity presents itself. Many do so. I did.

Thus what you get in a great deal of business journalism is corporate decision-making treated as palace politics with personal character the most important factor. This is what it would be in the legislature. The difference is that legislatures do not go bust and can afford long indulgence in petty squabbles. It is not often so in the executive suite. The result is that the real questions debated in the executive suite, questions of cost, efficiency, and capital expenditure are reported only after a clear decision has been made. Even then business journalists deal mostly with who made the decision and what it means for his career, followed by a great deal of idle stockbroker speculation about what it could mean for the share price.

All of this goes along with a note of moral high-mindedness. Sanctimony makes for easy copy. If God is with you who can stand against you? Familiarity with such things as return on invested capital are not required in order to side with God, particularly not when a question of environmental impact is involved and the greens are all clamouring to be heard. How fortunate that the greens, in particular, know the value to journalism of good visuals. Just record it all, pick the brightest bits, get the company public relations woman (she's waiting for your call) to give you the obligatory other side of the environmental angle, ignore what she says about cost efficiency (she probably won't anyway) and it's filed long before deadline. You'll be able to make it to your friend's birthday dinner after all. You'll even be in time for drinks. Just go with God and call the taxi.

One other reason it happens this way is that journalism marches to a faster beat than corporate affairs. Every day must have something new for print journalism, every hour for audio and video journalism and it is all event-driven. The fact that the sales trend continues generally up, just as it did last month, may interest investors but doesn't cut it for the news. There has to be a sales boom or a sales crash with some distinctly identifiable cause, or at least a plausible one. The result is a very short-sighted perspective of business affairs. Journalists look at the stitch, not the seam.

The worst of it shows up in the video feed. There it is all treated like football, complete with background drum beat if the pace is too slow. Highly presentable men and women (ever seen an ugly anchor?) interrupt each other to pontificate in sports idiom on the implications of a just-announced quarterly earnings number. Every now and then they must interview others but there are no layers to the onion of argument here. When those invited to the show try to explain some detail of why the earnings number may be unrepresentative they are soon cut off. The clock is ticking, attention in the viewing audience is waning, and another earnings number has just come in. The score has changed. What will the next move be on field?

You might think that this blather actually has value when you see it carried on screens in the lifts of all major buildings in the central business district but you will not find it given such prominence in the dealing room. It is there but the sound is turned off except, occasionally, if Mr Important of the day is scheduled to stand in front of a microphone somewhere. Otherwise the people on the desk have their attention on the real newsfeed they want – the Bloomberg screen. What it carries is not presenter gabble but numbers and charts.

And there you have the big mismatch between investment and journalism. Value in investment is best represented in numbers, not words. Share price movements, earnings breakdowns, book asset values and the like are numbers. The text is only in the headings. These are things best understood and best presented in lists, tables and charts.

This ain't Shakespeare, folks. Take that English degree somewhere else.

Most of all, hammer it into your head once again. It's in the price if it's in the press.

The B-school professor

I am not a big believer in higher education. Count me in for university-level professional studies in such fields as medicine, law and accountancy but count me out when it comes to a master's degree in creative writing and religious studies. What I have in mind when I think of such frivolities is the flight attendant who has subjected herself to sixteen years of education, all the way to a university degree in such subjects. Picture her now as she comes down the aisle, an hour after take-off, with her message to you from all this enormous effort of learning: 'Chicken or fish, Sir? We're out of the beef option.'

What a waste. We have far too much university education, far more than the available employment requires and if you want to tell me that learning is its own reward then here is my hat, turned over as you can see. I'm filling it with donations for that poor dupe who, on the advice of people like you, has blighted her life with student loans that she has no hope of repaying from the sort of work she can get for the education she has. Please give generously.

Of all these great educational wastes the one that concerns me here is the business school. Oh, let no-one say that its graduates cannot find jobs. They mostly do, and serially so at frequent intervals once they get on any hungry headhunter's candidate list. It is only my contention that little of what they learn in B-school will ever help them as corporate executives and, to the extent that it does, will only make them more proficient sharks in feeding on customers, employees and shareholders alike.

The basic premise of the B-school is that business administration is a skill with detailed rules and procedures that operate on common basis around the world. At one level it is certainly true. I don't think anyone should aspire to run a commercial enterprise without a solid grounding in book-keeping and corporate law, leave alone the basic nature of the enterprise itself.

But this is not the emphasis of the B-school. There it is rather on how to win. This in turn is a matter of initiating a range of winning strategies and adopting the correct responses to events. It is not always easy to do, the professor concedes. Sometimes one tactic works and sometimes not. What you must do is learn the different skills to adapt yourself properly to the specified circumstances.

The reason this is nonsense is that it is life itself. The range of winning strategies and correct responses is infinite. There are no hard and fast rules to apply to any given situation other than those imposed by law. There are only general principles of conduct and they are the ones you learned from the experiences of your life and from your upbringing as a child. If you have not learned them from your mother you will never learn them from strangers in B-school. Good judgement is not taught.

In practice what the B-school ethos leads to is corporate management that emphasises the interests of shareholders over those of employees and customers. This is what it does at its best. Often, however, it leads to emphasis of the interests of B-school trained executives over those of even the shareholders.

Which should be given more emphasis? Good question. Sometimes it is the customers, sometimes the staff, sometimes the shareholders but you look in vain for a Moses who has inscribed the answer in stone. Corporate decision-making is an art, not a science. The circumstances are inevitably just too dynamic, too bafflingly varied. Give yourself that grounding in book-keeping and corporate law and then pray that when you find yourself in times of trouble mother may come to you.

You certainly won't find that good judgement in so poor a substitute as a B-school professor who touts in the press every semester for a new crop of students to harvest for his budget pledges. These he then turns over to his teaching assistants so that he can get down to his real job of boosting his B-school's score of the number of unreadable papers published in academic journals. He has never held down a job outside of academia in his life. He certainly does not know.

You
Thus we come back to where we started – Who's the best stockpicker of them all? For the answer to that question

look once again in the mirror on the wall to which you posed the question.

You are.

Oh, nonsense, you say. How can I be? Others know much more about investment than I do, I never studied it, and it's not a field in which I work.

Of these three untruths, I particularly like the last one. You call it investment decision when you use money as the unit of account but it is really no different from the other daily decisions you make on how best to use your time and energy. Money just quantifies them on a common, single measuring stick of how much return you get for your effort, which then gives you a way of comparing these decisions to each other. It is more difficult to do in some endeavours than it is in others and it is not always precise but the underlying objective is the same. How much bang do you get for your time relative to other demands on your time, or for your calorific expenditure relative to your effort of calorific acquisition, or, to put it most simply, for your buck? Common-sense principles underlie it all. Investment is very much a field in which you work.

Think about it again. Investment is about enabling the development of enterprises in the hope that these enterprises will succeed rather than fail and that you will profit from the success. We are talking here about future events and we are all interested in future events. Why be a builder if the object isn't the completion of the house in the future? Why be a teacher if the object isn't little Jennifer with a degree in her hands in the future? Why be a pilot if the object isn't to get the flight safely to its destination in the future?

The difference here is that the people who do these things – the builder, the teacher and the pilot – know how to do them. Let us imagine a world, however, in which they do not. In this world the builder gives you a drawing of the completed house and says, 'There, that's my bit done. Here's my bill.' The teacher gives you a photo of a gradua-tion ceremony of the sort Jennifer might one day attend and says, 'Isn't it heartwarming?' The pilot says, 'This is the flight deck. You pull some levers, you push others, I think, and up you go. Now let me off before they pull away the airstairs.'

This is the world of investment. The experts don't know. They have expertise in plunking your money down for whatever you choose to buy but they cannot tell you whether that investment will go up or down in value, particularly not if you express it, as you should do, in terms of whether it will be up or down relative to other things you could do with your money.

Let me correct this statement. They can and do, in fact, tell you whether it will go up or down in any terms you care to choose. It's not difficult. Anyone can tell you such a thing. It's simple. You just say it. For instance, I can tell you that the moon is made of blue cheese. There, I have just done it. And now you can tell me that your hovercraft is full of eels.

Oh, how interesting. So was Monty Python's. It must be true then.

Imagine things another way. Let's say the question with
the house is not how to build it but whether its price in ten
years will rise by more or less than the prices of similar
houses on the market at that time relative to the prices of
each at present. Would you expect the builder to know?
Let's say the question with Jennifer is whether her first job
offer will give her a greater starting salary than any of the
two people immediately in front and behind her in the
eventual graduation line-up adjusted for any premium or
discount that people would put on Jennifer's chances at
present. Would the teacher know? Would anyone know?
I'm sure there is an equivalent question for the pilot. I won't
bother.

It is questions as imponderable as these with which a
market deals. Yet every one of them must be given an
answer. There is no market and no investment unless
someone puts up a price that represents his or her best guess
of the answer. And if people in general think this price too
high or too low then the price will move until opinion is
again in balance and the question as imponderable as it
ever was.

Yes, it is frustrating but it actually works to your benefit.
The more efficient a market, the more that these impon-
derables remain in balance, the better the prospect you have
of getting the fairest price anyone can get. You don't need
to read all those research reports, trawl through the stock
exchange announcements or crunch a vast array of spreadsheet numbers. The market has already done all this for

you and none can do it better. The range of choice is wide. Flip a coin and take what comes up.

I shall grant you that there are times when someone has an advantage over others in the market. Not all markets are always fully efficient. There is a good bit of this book still to go and much of it has to do with market inefficiencies. But I can tell you right now that the biggest inefficiencies usually arise from ill-considered government initiatives and that when the bureaucrat knocks so does opportunity. One person's folly is another's fortune. I can also tell you that those oh-so-clever manipulators who think they are smarter than the market and whose predations you so fear, very often leave the market smarting.

Whatever the case, no amount of research, yours or your investment adviser's, will tell you more about the present circumstances of the market than the market already reflects in its prices. Nor can all this study reveal the future. Your thoughts on what the future holds are as good as anyone's and they are what you must now rely on.

Thus, having made your choice, all you really need to do now is find someone with the technical competence to carry out your chosen transaction, your bank teller, let's say, or your personal investment adviser if you will. But I would go for the teller. She won't preach investment advice at you or overcharge you by quite as much.

No, I don't want to hear it. The mirror speaks truth. Let us have no more of this nonsense about how you have no investment experience. You study investment every day and all day long in questions of where you can best devote your scarce resources of time and effort to your best advantage. Every adult human being is an investment expert. Life is an investment exercise and you are your own best investment adviser.

No more of it, I say. This whingeing about your investment ignorance is just an abdication of your own intelligence. We can go on to look at the other foibles of how money and human initiative interact but it is you I am talking to, not any surrogate whom you are thinking of appointing.

CHAPTER 2

The tools of the trade

The thing is you have to take a view. You have to look at all the lessons of your own life and come to a decision on what goods and services society is likely to value as least as much in coming years as it values them now. In fact, if you hope to do better than others in investment, you have to ask yourself what goods and services society will value even more.

You do not really have a choice about taking a view. You do it by the fact of what you do with the money you save. You have taken a view even if you store it all as cash under a floorboard. By this deed you have either said that money is filthy and the use of it an offence to your moral standards (although you would have burnt it or given it away if you really believed this) or that the end of the world is nigh and ready cash will at least get you groceries when the end comes.

You would be wrong about this, by the way. The end of the world may indeed be nigh but, while you may then have ready cash, you will find no groceries in the shops to buy with this cash.

A savings deposit in a bank may be a little better, although not much. The interest it pays you will almost always be less than inflation, so that you will steadily lose the value of your money. You will also still not find groceries in the shops if the sky falls in. But at least your money cannot suddenly be lost to burglars or fire, as it could be if stuffed as cash under the floorboards. This still amounts to taking a view, however, if only that you think theft and fire are real threats to your savings.

You could, of course, try to avoid taking a view by putting all your money into a fund of country funds that holds all possible investments in every country it represents in exact proportion to the size of the markets in this overall fund. It is still a view but it is as neutral a view as you could take.

If you do it, however, you will be paying three levels of management fees on top of each other and thus in most years robbing yourself of all your gains. I think it makes sense to invest at least some money in funds rather than in specific stocks and bonds, particularly if you do not yet have much money, but I cannot see the investment sense in going into funds of funds of funds.

There is really no escaping it. When you invest you say by your choice of investment that the world in general has underestimated the potential of a particular class of goods or services for which there will in the future be at least as much demand as people at present think there will be and, hopefully, even more.

Be clear about this. You may take the view that there will be very great demand for soya burgers in the future. But if this is what everyone thinks and it turns out that there is only *good* demand, not *very great* demand, then your investment may decline in value. Although there is more demand than at present, very much more was expected and that expectation was not met. To do better than others do you not only have to be right about the view you take of what the future holds but it has to be different from what most other investors think.

What makes this so very difficult is that this 'group mind', the market, is already very good at knowing all that there is to know at present and pricing itself just right for this knowledge. Beating it is a grim prospect. And yet you must face up to it every time you invest because you have to take a view.

But, no, and I shall say it again, and again and again if you insist, your investment adviser faces no less grim a prospect than you do. His skill lies in how and where, not what and when, and he does not have your interests at heart as closely as you do. To avoid trouble for himself he will take the conventional view on almost anything he recommends to you, although invariably presenting it as a fresh idea, and he will charge you extra fees for it. Getting others to tell you what to do is a cop-out.

What nonetheless makes money for you on most occasions is that economies in peacetime, operating under sound public administration, mostly grow in accumulated wealth. Investment markets reflect this fact. Your choice may be poor and yet the value of your investment rise. You may not do as well overall as others but the general gain from the benefits of economic growth have still often been enormous and you certainly do much better than the mattress or the savings account. Fortune favours the bold. Be content.

Do not think, however, that this gift of economic growth is necessarily yours by right. As a simple exercise, the World Bank calculates that the size of the world economy in the year 1000 was US$6.35 billion in inflation-adjusted 1990 terms and that in the year 2000 it was US$41,016 billion on the same basis. It looks like a big difference but it works out to an average economic growth rate of just under 0.9 per cent a year, that's all.

Perhaps the world has gone to a permanent basis of higher economic growth and this millennial figure is much too low for the future. Then again, perhaps human environmental offences will soon come round to bite us and world economic growth will be far short of even that 0.9 per cent a year. I caution you only not to be too ambitious in what you expect economic growth to do for you. Enjoy your windfalls but treat them as gifts from heaven.

And I advise you to pay special favour to the dull and boring when you take a view. These are frequently attributes of the best choices you could make. I recall one fund manager of considerable insight once saying that he liked the sort of company any fool could run on the grounds that sooner or later some fool would. Funny and true. He also had it as an attribute of an excellent prospect that the company headquarters be located far from any airport so that few investment commentators would visit it. I see the point. Unrecognised value is likely to be found where others don't want to look. If people find it thrilling, depend on it that the price will have taken full account of the thrills.

I shall not make it a rule that dull is good but I do think dull investments are more often better than those that appear exciting, personally appealing or particularly innovative. Your object is to make money, not buy new gadgets for the living room or kitchen. What's good in your pantry is not necessarily good in your portfolio.

But how can you know what is good for your portfolio?

Time to open the toolbox. First, however, the big proviso. You may find that these tools do not help you much. They do not even help investment professionals much. The market has already long taken account of the measurements they make. Don't expect it to be otherwise for you. If you do not find that the market has mostly measured it right then you may safely assume that you have mostly measured it wrong.

What is more, no measurement you can make has any meaning except in the context of similar measurements of other investments in similar circumstances.

Above all, few of the tools in this toolbox have any worthwhile purpose except when used on the proper tool bench. May you give this tool bench more respect than many investment advisers I have encountered. Let me introduce it:

The accounts

You don't always find a company's annual report and accounts carried prominently on its website, and with reason. Once a year the company is required to show its all in this document. Who really wants to strip naked to the public?

I do not think you really need to read an annual report from back to front, as one friend of mine recommends, but you can safely ignore the first two-thirds of self-praise and social responsibility blather. The important bit, the accounts, is at the end. If you have come this far, you may now have a question – How does one read a balance sheet?

Before we address it, let me ask you a question about yourself. Are you the sort of person to wave your hands in front of your face when the term 'balance sheet' comes up and say, 'Tell me later. I never really did any courses on that. It hasn't been my thing.'

Is that the kind of person you are? Good. That's the kind of person I am addressing. Here is what you must bear in mind. Published balance sheets are compiled for people like you by accountants who have spent years learning the intricacies of accounting so that you do not have to do so. What you get in published accounts is the standard easy-to-read format. You need take no courses to decipher it. Stop denying your own intelligence.

Now look again. The first thing you see in the accounts is not usually the balance sheet but the profit and loss account. Sit for ten minutes and look closely. Is it really so mysterious? The P&L account shows you how much money the company took in through sales and then how much of it was paid out to others – staff costs, supplies, interest charges, amortisation, tax and so on.

Amortisation? Turn three pages and you will find a long section headed 'Major Accounting Policies'. They say 'Major' but the point is to answer almost every question you could have, major and minor. Look also at the first mention of amortisation in the P&L account. It carries a number in small superscript. Flip past Major Accounting Policies until you find a section with this number. It will tell you even more about amortisation. Still not satisfied? Ask Google.

Right, back we go to the P&L account. After all the costs and deductions we get to after-tax profit and finally to earnings (profit) per share. Congratulations. You now understand the basics of reading a P&L account.

And now the balance sheet. Turn the page. The top half of the balance sheet, assets, lists by value all the things the company owns from the most difficult to sell and turn into cash down all the way to the easiest, cash itself. Add them up and you get total assets. The bottom half of the balance sheet, liabilities, lists where all the money came from to buy all these things, mostly debt and money subscribed by the shareholders for their shares. Add them all up and you get total capital employed. It is the same figure as total assets. That's why they call it a balance sheet. It balances.

Questions? Back you go to Major Accounting Policies and Notes to the Accounts. Back to Google if you must. Are you intrigued, for instance, by the murkiness of executive pay? The Notes to the Accounts can dispel the murk for you. They will tell you exactly what the directors and senior executive are paid right down to the full details of their share options. You have never told the world as much about your own income. As I say, naked to view.

To the tools then. The ones I describe here are mostly for use with the stock market but you start with them anyway if you are looking at other investments. They may come with different names but the concepts are the same.

P/E

The price-to-earnings ratio, also known as the earnings multiple or just P/E, is the most common measuring stick you will find in the tool box. The concept is simple. Divide the share price by the annual earnings or profits per share and you get a multiple. A stock with a share price of $50 and earnings per share of $5 is trading at 10 times earnings, usually expressed as 10x.

How nice to know, you say. Obviously, however, a stand-alone figure of 10x has about as much investment value to you as the factoid that the airspeed velocity of an unladen swallow is 11 metres per second.

Context is everything with P/E, starting with the context of the 'E' part of the P/E, which is not actually as simple as it appears. Do we use last year's reported earnings or this year's forecast earnings?

Last year's reported earnings, say some people, because the historic figure is at least accepted fact and anyone can cook up fiction for prospects this year. This year's forecast earnings, say other people, because we are investing for a future return, not a return in the past. Take your own choice. Most investors opt for the forecast earnings. Be aware only that if you see the earnings described as trailing or LTM (last twelve months) then you have the historic figure and if you hear the forecast earnings introduced as 'Well, personally, I think they could do at least. . . .' then a second opinion may be worthwhile.

Next question: Just what constitutes earnings? There is a lot of wiggle room here. Some people deduct only immediate operating costs from total revenues to arrive at what they call a profit. Accepted practice when calculating a P/E, however, is to be hardnosed. Earnings means after-tax earnings, the after, after, after, most conservative number. Thus, if someone talks about a pre-tax or operating profit multiple, it is not what most people mean by P/E. Be careful about comparing it with P/E numbers you may have in mind for other stocks.

And another: earnings per share (you will mostly see it shortened to just EPS) is the result of a separate calculation in which you divide total after-tax profits by the number of shares the company has outstanding. This should be no trouble, you say. The company has already done it for us. It has announced both a total earnings and an EPS number.

Perhaps it has given you several EPS numbers including one called 'fully diluted', which is the lowest figure of the bunch. What this means is that the senior executives have awarded themselves share options, the right to buy a fixed number of company shares in the future at an already determined price, and you are being told what the EPS will be if the rights are all exercised and the shares all issued. Count on it that they will be. The executives did not give themselves these rights just to leave them lying around on the floor.

In moderation, share options are not a bad thing. They incentivise the company's executives to work hard to keep the share price up, which should be just fine by you. But it may happen that these executives expect to be head-hunted to a new firm within a few years and their only objective is to max out the share price and cash in their options just at the time they leave. The devil then take the hindmost of those who are still holding the shares and find all the company's weaknesses suddenly become prominent. That hindmost could be you. Big share-option schemes are an indicator of thieves at work.

Note also that what we have here is only an EPS number for historic earnings. By how many shares shall we divide the forecast earnings to arrive at a forecast EPS? I have rarely seen two people come to exactly the same answer. Aside from the way that executives can loot the company treasury through share option schemes, active companies use their shares to make acquisitions and this involves timing adjustments for earnings per share. We shall not bother. My point is only that the 'E' part of P/E is not quite as hard a number as you might think it.

And now let us put this in the context of other investments you could make. Starting with the most general, we need a figure for what might be called the average yield of the currency in which your investment is denominated. This is also called the risk-free rate of return. At its simplest, this is the lowest interest rate at which a perfectly sound entity can borrow money for the medium term. In the United States take the coupon (interest rate) on a ten-year treasury (US dollar federal government bond). Easy. And now do it for the Philippine peso.

Yes, tough, I admit it and while you may be able to define it to the second place to the right of the decimal for the US dollar you will be scratching your head as to whether or not it is in double digits to the left of the decimal for the peso. Nonetheless, the market value of investments in Philippine peso rests on assumptions about the average yield of the peso. It is just another one of those investment puzzles in which the individual does not have a clue to the answer but the overall market does.

What individuals do know, however, is that the yield figure is higher for the peso than it is for the US dollar and that there are good reasons for this. To name just a few, the Philippines is not as politically stable, its creaky financial markets are underdeveloped, its society is more polarised and the peso is not generally rated a strong currency. It all makes money tighter, which is reflected in higher interest rates or, for our purposes, a higher average yield.

This affects the stock market as much as it does borrowings. A P/E ratio is really only the reverse of a percentage calculation. To say that a stock is trading at 20 times earnings is the same as saying that it is trading at a 5 per cent earnings yield. And as sure as water is wet, you will not find a stock market trading on average at a 5 per cent earnings yield if the average yield of the rest of the economy is 20 per cent. To phrase it another way, the market will not trade at 20 times earnings if other financial assets in the currency are trading at an average of 5 times earnings. Investments in any currency are very much related in their pricing relative to their income.

But let us limit the range of comparisons for now. Armed with a P/E number for your stock, the first thing you ask yourself is how it compares with other stocks listed on the market. If it is lower than the market average you may tell yourself that you have a cheap stock and a worthwhile investment candidate.

Except, except, except. . . . What if it has a lower P/E than the overall market but a higher P/E than its sector of the market? In every market some sectors trade at a lower P/E than other sectors because, for instance, they are considered to be in rust belt industries that are in demise or because their earnings are considered highly insecure. Is your stock still cheap if it trades at a premium to its sector?

What if the P/E of your stock is lower only because it enjoys a sudden blush of earnings that no-one expects to continue? What if, conversely, it is higher because it has suffered an earnings slump from which most people expect it to recover? What if it's lower/higher because this is the kind of stock market in which family control is still a major factor and the market has a high/low opinion of the controlling family? What if any number of factors that affect the relative P/E of a stock, including political developments or the phases of the moon, which in stock markets dominated by Chinese investors have traditionally had a noticeable effect in the run-up to the Chinese New Year.

As a rule, the closer you look the more likely you are to find that the market has reasons for pricing the stock at just the P/E at which it stands. If you do not find it so, then think again because you are probably wrong. The P/E ratio is a tool that can very occasionally alert you to unrecognised value. Mostly it alerts you to how well the market has already recognised value.

EBITDA

EBITDA stands for earnings before interest, tax, depreciation and amortisation. Be wary. It is not a ratio, just a way of defining earnings. It is in common use and it is the wrong measure for you as a portfolio investor.

The difficulty lies with the understanding most of us have of what constitutes a profit. We think of profit as what is left for the shareholder after all other obligations have been settled. Interest payments do not qualify as profit under this understanding. Lenders may defer their demands for interest but only temporarily and the unpaid portion of interest due just goes into making the overall debt greater. The same holds true for tax. And while a company can temporarily ignore that its vehicle fleet, for instance, is growing older, sooner or later it will have to replace that fleet. Depreciation is a way of providing for this by setting money aside for new vehicles from what would otherwise be profits. You ignore all this as a company executive at the peril of your company's future.

But what if the company is already in peril, scratching to stay alive, hoping that some new product line or marketing hype will restore its financial health? It can then tell lenders to stop making their demands for interest payments or risk losing all. It needs to pay no profits tax as it makes no profits. It can ignore the need for renewal of the vehicle fleet as this will only be a problem next year at the earliest and the problem at the moment is whether it can meet next month's payroll or have the workforce walk off the job. In such circumstances EBITDA makes sense as a measure of corporate viability.

This is also the way a receiver looks at things in a corporate bankruptcy. If he assumes that the shareholders are plumb out of luck and will get nothing back and if he assumes the absolute minimum level of capital investment needed to keep the company teetering along, will there be any income left to pay the unsecured creditors a small percentage of what is owed them? If so, perhaps this company can stay in business and hope for a miracle.

And then you have the smooth-talking pedlar of fast ideas (oops, sorry, I mean professional investment adviser) who invokes EBITDA because if he tells you that the stock he is pushing is priced at 200x earnings you will just walk away. With EBITDA he may get it down to 40x and still just possibly snare you. If not, he might tell you that this particular sector of the market is priced at multiples of sales revenues rather than any notion of profits and now it is just 20x. Walk away.

Bureaucrats love EBITDA for this reason, too. Not for them the arduous work of making a sale, of convincing the public of its own free will to part with money, not when they can issue tax demands or borrow money easily because governments never fail (hah!). Sometimes, however, bureaucrats find themselves having to think about money as others do, for instance when building a commuter railway that charges passenger fares. They cannot offer a completely free service to the public. Taxi and bus companies will complain. But invariably, and I really do mean without fail, it turns out that the railway cannot make a profit. Private taxi and bus companies can make a profit but a railway built at public expense cannot. How strange.

EBITDA to the rescue. The bureaucrat writes off all the construction expenditure as an outright loss, although he will rarely use the word 'loss' to his public. From this it follows that there is also no need to make interest payments on any of the money raised from the public purse. He next gives the railway a long or permanent tax holiday. Finally, he pretends that there is no wear and tear at all on a railway and thus no need to make provision for depreciation. Mix it all in with passenger numbers projected at twice the prevailing rate and magic arises. The railway is profitable. Who'd a thunk it.

In my view it is entirely understandable that desperate directors, company receivers and self-deluding bureaucrats look at things this way. Are you one of these? No? Then if you hear too much talk of EBITDA, jump.

Price to cash flow
I think of it as EBITDA lite. With this metric you take operating cash flow, which means that, unlike EBITDA, you do not ignore interest payments and tax. They are real expenditures and you treat them as such. You ignore only items not involving the movement of funds. This means mostly depreciation and amortisation. The company does not actually pay out any money when it provides in its accounts for wear and tear of the vehicle fleet. It makes a deduction from operating profits but it still has use of the money. There are other examples of such free cash flow adjustments, for instance the treatment of profits attributable to minority shareholders. We won't bother here.

You do not have to work out what this cash flow is per share. It is given to you in the accounts under the heading Sources and Applications of Funds, which usually comes right after the balance sheet. Now all that you have to do is divide the present share price by this cash flow per share figure and you have your price to cash flow ratio.

What wonders. It is lower than the P/E ratio. The stock you are considering looks even cheaper now. No wonder your stockbroker said you should look at things this way.

But what do you really have? You are pretending that vehicle fleet will never wear out and so you can thus ignore depreciation. It is a metric the company can fall back on if it has immediate pressing financial difficulties or cannot find people to lend it money for new acquisitions.

Alternatively, talk of cash flow may tell you that the company is being circled by financier sharks looking for a feeding opportunity called a leveraged buy-out. Prospects of an LBO can indeed help keep a share price up but you are very unlikely to spot an LBO prospect before the sharks do so. If they succeed in feeding you will never get near their prey and if you are already in the stock you are their feed unless you get out at their price.

Price to cash flow is a ratio for corporate financiers to consider. You are not one of these. If you hear too much of it, jump.

ROIC-WACC

Here is one that I really like and is favoured by many analysts. Alas, it no longer works.

My great delight in it comes from the time that the Hong Kong government decided years ago to list its superb metro system, the Mass Transit Railway, on the stock market. One of the MTR's big attractions is that Hong Kong commuters can ride on it from one end of Hong Kong to the other, a journey of nearly two hours, for less than the cost of a one-stop hop on the London Underground.

This, however was also a weakness in the pricing of the stock. The government wanted a listing value of HK$100 billion but the investment bankers said that its low earnings justified a value of only HK$25 billion. The difference was made up by turning it into a property development company with an infusion of HK$75 billion worth of land on which building height limitations had been removed.

It was still thought, however, that this sleight of hand might not prove enough and that the listing might still prove difficult. All those brought into the exercise were therefore told to exert themselves mightily, including the investment analyst at the bank chosen to lead the issue. He wrote a glowing report of almost 200 pages, praising the stock throughout. The lawyers and public relations people who checked his every word all nodded in approval. Good job.

What they missed showed up about three quarters of the way down a one-page table of forecast figures in the middle of the report. The numbers that followed the heading, ROIC-WACC, all bore a minus notation for as far into the future as the analyst made his forecasts.

In just that one line of a language that his minders could not read he had let his true views be known to his fellow financial analysts – 'Hey, guys, this one's a dog!'

Why?

ROIC-WACC stands for return on invested capital less weighted average cost of capital. It poses an essential first question – does this enterprise generate more money from its investment than it puts into the investment? Any investment is obviously only worthwhile if you get more out of it than you put into it. If less, then you are destroying capital and you should get out or the investment will eventually destroy *you*. Bear in mind here that this metric takes account, on both sides of the equation, of the debt a company has taken on as well as the money raised from shareholders. It is a comprehensive metric. Get ROIC-WACC right and you can dispense with most other metrics of investment value.

Unfortunately, this wonderful tool now breaks in your hand. The problem lies in the WACC part of the equation. It assumes that you assign a percentage cost to share capital in the same way that you assign an interest rate to debt capital.

This may seem counter-intuitive at first. No-one has made any promises to shareholders. The company has an obligation to pay its creditors interest on borrowings from them but shareholders are entitled only to cross their fingers and hope it all works. Tough luck for them if it does not. There are no shoulders for them to cry on.

The more modern understanding, however, is that this won't do. Shareholders have expectations that cannot be scorned. They can sell up and run out if they are not happy, which does a company no good. Best keep them happy. It is not only fair to them, and not only makes strict commercial sense but it is not wise to anger big investment funds that control trillions of dollars.

What percentage cost figure, however, should analysts assign to share capital? It was always a difficult question but usually, and acceptably, answered with reference to the percentage yield on a long-term US dollar treasury.

And then the US Federal Reserve Board got busy with a form of monetary monkeying called quantitative easing, reducing interest rates (and bond yields) to far below where the market could have been expected to put them. This makes a mockery of any calculation of the cost of share capital. It makes even the interest cost element of WACC doubtful. A valuable tool has been lost. The weighted average cost of capital can no longer be determined within any useful range. Alas.

But there is still one remaining use to this tool. Do you wish to look good in the company of investment know-it-alls? Just nod astutely when a stock you recognise is being discussed and say that, when you looked at it, an ROIC of minus two over weighted capital did not give you much prospect of an appreciation of shareholder value. No-one can prove you wrong. You can pick any figure you want for weighted capital cost. You always come out looking mighty informed. Congratulations.

ROE

Return on Equity is another commonly cited metric and, again, not one really suited to your purposes. It measures net profits as a percentage of equity or of shareholders' funds, as it is often expressed in the balance sheet. The required numbers are all available from the accounts for the historic calculation. Remember only when working out an ROE that your shareholders' funds figure should be the average of what it was at the beginning and at the end of the financial year.

Why is it not useful for you?

Simple. Shareholders' funds, when expressed on a per share basis, almost certainly do not represent what you paid for the share. It rather represents what the company paid for its assets or the value later assigned to those assets through a professional valuation. It gives the original shareholders a good idea of how much bang they have for the buck they originally contributed.

You, however, are not an original shareholder. You came later or you are only looking at the share now. What you are being asked to pay is what the market thinks these assets are worth at present. It could be a wildly different figure. The company's ROE is not yours.

ROE also suffers from the drawback that, although it incorporates profits made through debt financing, it only shows them as a percentage of shareholders' funds. It does not really answer the question of how well judged the company's reliance on debt financing has been. And it certainly does not tell you how good this return has been relative to the overall cost of the company's capital. Changes in ROE from year to year can give you a rough indication of whether profitability is improving or deteriorating but it is, once again, primarily a tool for the company's finance director and its lenders.

ROE has one additional big disadvantage that is best explained in another metric.

Price to book

Here is the easy way of working out what a stock is worth: First, look up the figure for shareholders' funds again. It is also referred to as book value or just the 'book'. Next, divide that by the number of shares and compare this to the share price. You now have the price-to-book ratio, a a measure of whether the company is worth more or less than its share price.

It is an unreliable measure.

The difficulty lies in how the company's accountant sets a value on the 'book'. Most times he just uses the depreciated cost of the company's assets. Thus if the company has paid $30,000 for a new car for its vehicle fleet and this car is now one year old, he will look up his depreciation schedule and find that new cars are depreciated to zero over five years on a straight line basis. He will then put in a depreciation charge of $6,000 on this year-old car and its book value will be $24,000. It makes sense. All well and good.

But what if the asset is a piece of land acquired ten years ago for, let us say, $10 million, and not only have real-estate values generally shot up since that time but the area has become trendy and local authorities have proved happy to bend their zoning regulations to accommodate trendiness there. The land could easily be sold to a developer for $100 million now. At what value should this land then be carried in the balance sheet? Keep it at cost and the shareholders' funds entry will give you too low a figure for the value of the company.

This problem of land valuation is exacerbated in former British colonies because of an anomaly of colonial administration, which is a fascinating story in itself but we won't go into it here. I frequently had to deal with it in Hong Kong as an investment analyst, however, laboriously working out estimates of the market value of a company's property holdings and comparing these with the balance sheet costs in order to arrive at what we called the discount from net asset value, i.e. a price to book.

It was then resolved that land and building values should be restated every year at a directors' (unreliable) or professional (semi-reliable) estimate of market value. The difference from cost would be carried in a special reserve but not treated as profit unless these assets were actually sold. Prudent accounting principle No. 1 says that you do not book a profit unless you have it in your hands but you book a loss if you see one coming. All well and good.

And then new standards were imposed by the big international accounting houses, under the Generally Accepted Accounting Principles, to say that these valuation differences should instead be carried immediately to the profit and loss account every year. The inevitable result was more violent up and down swings of profitability in the property sector. Not well and good.

Valuation headaches that never have a fully satisfactory outcome are even worse with intangible assets. What is the

value of the intellectual property rights to a doll that has
suddenly become a marketing hit? They will be much
greater than the development costs of the doll. If you buy
the rights you will have crystallised the value and can
incorporate this purchase price in your balance sheet. But
what if the hit value of the doll suddenly vanishes as quickly
as it arose? How long can you continue to carry that hit
value in your balance sheet? Should you write it down and
book a loss? If so, when and to what value will you write it
down? There are no good definite answers. Accountants
try to make hard-and-fast rules for such eventualities but
they never satisfy. It is the basic flaw at the heart of both
the ROE and price-to-book ratios. You just cannot get your
fingers firmly around that 'E' or 'book' part. Thus repeat
after me – Value is not price is not cost. Keep repeating it.

There is, however, another way of looking at this. No
asset aside from cash has an intrinsic value. The value of
any asset to a company is only the company's ability to
generate earnings from the asset. And there is an excellent
measure of how good any company is at doing this. It is
called the share price. A price-to-book ratio does not tell
you whether the share price is too high or too low relative
to the book. It rather tells whether the stated value of the
book is too high or too low relative to the share price. The
share price is a much better arbiter of value than shareholders' funds are. Unfortunately, whilst this form of report
card may be of considerable value to a company's executives, it does nothing for you as an outside investor.

I can actually refine this understanding a little further. As a sometime properties analyst in Hong Kong I found that some property stocks consistently traded at much steeper discounts from their appraised net asset values than did others. One in particular went public on the promise of two new hotels it was building. After the listing was successfully achieved it leased both hotels to the chairman's private family firm for twenty years on a derisory rent. It avoided legal sanctions, but did not get away with it on the market. The stock never traded at better than a 40 per cent discount from net asset value and always had difficulty raising new money. Another developer who always left some crumbs on the table for his followers routinely saw his stock trade at a premium to net-asset value and had but to say the word to have investors falling over themselves with offers of money. Price-to-book is sometimes a good measure of executive competence or honesty. But, once again, the truth of the appraisal lies in the share price, not the book.

Profit margin

Here is another example of a profitability measure that is useful to a company's executives but of little use to you. Let me introduce it with a riddle:

> Question: When is 1 per cent more than 30 per cent?

Answer: When it's on the shop shelf and not the shop itself.

It does not trouble a grocer that the profit margin on an item he carries is very slim so long as it turns over rapidly. In fact, he does very well most times to enjoy a net profit margin of one per cent. If he earns five cents on a $5 bottle of soft drink but these bottles fly off the shelf so fast that he replaces them every week then his profit margin on his rolling cost of soft drink sales is more than 50 per cent a year.

And now let us take the case of the developer who has built the shopping mall in which the grocer operates. What with all the difficulties of land acquisition, council building approval and regulatory oversight he might find that it has taken him three years between the date that he committed his money and the date that all the shops were finally leased out and he could sell the mall to other investors. He may at the end of this time have earned $130 million for total costs of $100 million but, spread over three years, this comes to an annualised profit margin of only 10 per cent. The grocer has done much better.

So why do we inflexibly set the length of the standard financial accounting period at twelve months when for some companies the most appropriate period would be one week and for others three years?

Your answer is that we do it because it takes one year for planet Earth to make one revolution around the Sun. Don't ask me why astronomy should be made the arbiter of the standard product turnover cycle.

I also have other quibbles about profit margins. For instance, grocers often delay payments to their suppliers so that they can amass money for 'treasury' operations, which means investing that money in short-term instruments for profit. Do we include these profits when calculating the profit margin on soft drink sales? Should we?

Grocers track their profit margin closely for changes and for comparison with other grocers but the rest of us will never develop as keen an eye for what they see and, in any case, we have more than grocers to consider. For us, the comparison of profit margins between different sectors is a comparison of apples to oranges. What's more, if there is any significance in it, count on the share price to make its adjustments long before you notice it.

Dividend yield

Years ago I escorted a group of senior American fund managers to a meeting with a big power utility in Hong Kong and one of the first questions that came up was why the utility had raised its dividend by 20 per cent a year for several years.

'Oh, that's simple,' said the utility's man. 'China takes over here in 1997 and we wanted to make sure that in the intervening time we could restore to our shareholders all the investment they had made in case this handover doesn't go well.'

Jaws dropped at the table and the leader of the group then turned to one of his colleagues and said, 'Now go stick that into your dividend discount model and see if you don't buy the whole company.'

Ah, yes, the dividend discount model, gone and departed, alas. The idea here is that the only money you truly receive from your investment in the shares of a company is the dividend the company pays you. If you sell the stock you also receive money but this is from the buyer of the stock, not the company. The only other circumstance in which you can receive money from the company is its dissolution. But then the company is probably bankrupt and you will get nothing.

So let us turn to the simple dividend discount model to see how much a share is worth. First, you make a long-term forecast of the company's future dividend payments, including any growth you might reasonably expect in them.

Next, ask yourself how much you would be willing to pay today for the right to receive $100 in a year's time. Let's say it is $93. The difference, 7 per cent, is your discount rate.

Now call up the financial calculator on your spreadsheet, pick out the option called 'net present value', enter the numbers for your dividend stream and your discount in the spaces provided and press the enter key. Presto, you have what this dividend stream is worth to you today. If it is more than the present share price you have a good argument for buying the stock.

This is to say, you once had a good argument. But once again it has been destroyed by the monetary monkeying to which central banks around the world, particularly in the United States and Europe, have been prone all this century. Ultra-low interest rates have so distorted discount rates that they no longer make valuation sense. Together with the effect of dividend taxes, this has also discouraged the payment of dividends. Another valuable tool has been lost.

And yet I would not disregard dividends. To my way of thinking, the payment of a regular dividend is an explicit recognition by a company of its responsibility to its shareholders.

I recognise the argument that there may be times when a company can do better with its money than pay part of it out to shareholders. This may or may not be true but there is no way of knowing whether it is. Just for starters, the argument assumes that company directors know how well their shareholders would do with the money if they, rather than the company, held it. I think it immediately obvious that no-one could know any such thing, which makes the argument pointless. The decision, in any case, is for the shareholders, not the directors, to make. If the shareholders think it true then they will put their dividend money right back into the company.

But this is not what concerns me here. What concerns me is rather that I find myself uncomfortable with companies that scorn dividends. I happen to think that there is just something more trustworthy about directors who say, 'Hey, here's something for you.' It bespeaks an understanding of corporate purpose as going beyond immediate returns alone, an understanding that I think is crucial to sustained long-term success.

So do keep your eye on the dividend yield (annual dividend payments as a percentage of the share price). It's a hard figure, unlike so many other valuation ratios and it's money in your hands.

I understand that you may not think it quite enough on its own to justify the present share price. With the destruction of the dividend discount model, I cannot now demonstrate otherwise but I can still suggest one test. Go back over the share price record of a solid dividend payer over the last ten years and adjust that record upwards throughout for its dividends. You will be surprised at how well the stock has really done in these total-return terms.

Debt to equity

Gearing, they often call it, and beware if you hear the word from an investment adviser. It is your job to decide how much risk you want to take, not his. If you want to add to that risk by investing with borrowed money, well, it's your funeral if it all goes wrong, while your adviser collects his fee regardless.

Things are not quite the same when you look at corporate gearing. Every corporation wants quick access to short-term debt for times when the incomings come in slower than the outgoings go out. Sometimes a company also spots an acquisition opportunity that will not last long.

The only way to take advantage of it may be to borrow the necessary money. This is all good operating procedure. Debt is part of corporate life. The question is what an optimal level of corporate debt might be.

And the answer is that there is no answer. As with so many questions in finance, it all depends; in this case mostly on the relative costs of equity and debt financing.

Put yourself in the position of a finance director debating with himself how to fund the purchase of a new asset for which the company does not have enough ready money at hand. He needs, let us say, $10 million and finds that he can borrow this at an annual interest cost of 5 per cent. Next, he works out how many new shares he would have to issue to raise that $10 million through an equity route and finds that it would require a 7 per cent addition to share capital. The choice is obvious. Why dilute the existing shareholders' interests by 7 per cent with new shares when he can reduce that effective cost to 5 per cent with debt? He chooses the debt route.

Sometimes, of course, there may still be reasons to go with equity, for instance if the company already has a very high ratio of debt to equity, say 200 per cent, and the finance director believes that interest rates are going up. Then a question of the company's financial health may intrude on his calculations. But in normal circumstances the choice is a matter of relative costs and a 200 per cent debt-to-equity ratio may be just fine if interest costs are lower than equity costs and returns on capital are higher than the costs of capital. In some sectors, investment banking for instance, a 200 per cent debt-to-equity ratio can be considered unusually low. Of course, it helps at such times if one of the investment bank's former directors has been appointed secretary of the national treasury and has both the means and the will to rescue his former colleagues from reckless borrowings. Could it happen? Oh, well now.

But the corporate viewpoint is not one you can take in personal finance. You cannot issue shares in yourself to the general public, at least not without becoming one of the great human curiosities of the age. Your only equity alternative to debt is your own personal savings. Yet you may be quite ready to see your own personal debt-to-equity ratio go as high as 1,000 per cent. People frequently do it when they take on mortgages to buy their homes. What matters then is whether your income is great enough to cover your mortgage costs and still allow you to live comfortably.

Take note in this context of how national debt, as opposed to corporate debt, is most often measured. There is no accepted figure for a nation's equity and so national debt cannot be compared to national equity. Instead it is most often compared to annual gross domestic product. This compares apples to oranges. Debt is a balance-sheet figure but GDP is a sort of truncated cash-flow figure that has no exact counterpart in corporate accounts. One measures a quantity at a set moment in time (debt) and the other a flow over a defined period (GDP).

It is a bit like comparing a reservoir to a stream of water flowing into it and saying that the reservoir holds as much water as the annual inflow from the stream. The stream to reservoir ratio on this basis is thus 100 per cent. But take the flow over three months and the stream to reservoir ratio becomes 25 per cent. A civic official wondering how long it will take this reservoir to fill up will not make the mistake of saying that the stream and reservoir are the same thing because they both involve water. Yet many people make that mistake when comparing debt to GDP.

If you want to measure them on the same basis you must do either one of two things. The first is to estimate the annual interest costs on the debt as a percentage of annual GDP. The second is to treat GDP as a continuing stream of earnings and estimate its discounted balance-sheet value that way. Either of these two exercises will allow you a valid comparison and, in each case, the resulting ratio will indicate a much lower dependence on debt than the simplistic debt to GDP number gives you.

The biggest problem with national debt, however, is not how high it is but how well it is invested for the good of all. National debt, unfortunately, is rarely as prudently invested as corporate or personal debt.

The Shakespearean adage of 'Neither a borrower nor a lender be' was all very well for its time but debt is an inescapable part of both personal and corporate finance today. My point is first of all that you should be wary of applying guidelines on personal debt to corporate finance and, secondly, that there is no benchmark for a corporate debt-to-equity ratio. It can be judged too high or too low only in the context of what debt financing would cost relative to equity financing, whether interest rates are trending up or down and how sound the company's finances are otherwise. Fill in the blanks of this equation and the debt-to-equity ratio may give you a hint of whether you have a good investment prospect.

But it will only be a hint. If you think it gives you a clear signal you have probably filled in the blanks with the wrong answers. That's the way with the investment business. It's very hard to be smarter than the market.

Yield to redemption

All the tools I have described so far are related primarily to the stock market.

This one is purely for the bond market.

Assume a $100 bond that you bought for $100 and pays an annual coupon of $5. Your yield on your cost of this bond is thus 5 per cent.

Now assume that it is still a $100 bond but you bought it at a fire-sale price of $80. Your coupon rate is still $5 but this is no longer your yield. That $5 on your purchase price of $80 equates to a yield of 6.25 per cent.

There is more to consider. When this bond matures you will get the $100 principal back. You not only get a 6.5 per cent yield on your cost until maturity but you get $20 more than the $80 you paid. How much is that extra $20 worth to you now in annual percentage terms until maturity? What will it be if you add in that 6.25 per cent yield figure?

Don't trouble your head with it. Just call up a bond calculator on whatever digital device you have to hand, plug in your numbers for prices, coupon, maturity date and principal amount and out will come a figure. It is called a yield to redemption, it is the annual all-in percentage payback, and on a $100 bond priced at $80 it is likely to be a high figure.

But, stop. What if that $80 price on a $100 bond means that the market thinks this bond may go into default and you will get much less than $100 for it at maturity, perhaps nothing at all. What do the ratings agencies say? Is there a credit default swap on this bond and what does its price tell you?

Headache, headache, headache – all made worse by the fact that you are competing with the career bond dealer. He is surrounded at his desk by banks of screens powered by high-speed processors working off automatic data feeds. He can do it all much faster than you can do it, with much more precision and with a much greater perspective across the entire bond market.

Why compete with the bond desk? Best do your bond investing through bond funds, I say, unless you have very good reason to take a view otherwise. You rarely will.

Cap rate

This is short for capitalisation rate and when you hear the term you are dealing with real-estate investment. It expresses annual net rental receipts as a percentage of the price of a building. At least, this is what it is if you have just bought the building or have set yourself a price that you are willing to pay for it. More commonly it is a calculation that management agents make when the owners for whom they act ask: 'What do you think my building is worth these days?'

Then the agent works it backward. He takes what he thinks is the prevailing cap rate in the market and derives a price from it. His owners then say, 'Wow!' or something like it, which reflects the fact that real-estate prices in most developed markets have risen astronomically for the last fifty years.

Cap rate is essentially the same thing as a price-to-earnings ratio or an earnings yield. The difference is only that you need to be a little more definite about what is included. Most people take it as an EBITDA calculation. They deduct from rental receipts all management, insurance and upkeep costs plus local government rates but they make no provision for depreciation, interest charges or taxes.

Do it the EBITDA way and real-estate returns can look quite attractive compared with other investments. But now do it the fully costed way by asking yourself how much money you really get to keep for yourself at the end of the day. Suddenly the picture is not quite so attractive any longer.

I shall repeat my general advice. Real-estate investment is a headache if you do it directly in a small way. Unless you like fixing your tenant's leaky taps at midnight and dealing with lawyers' letters from stroppy neighbours, wait until you are at least into six zeros. Until then do it through real-estate securities or just stay out of this sector entirely.

Oh, yes, one more thing. Don't do time shares. Just don't. They are a grand way of paying far too much for a vacation home and giving your returns to others while taking on their risk.

In short. . . .

Money does not grow on trees, does not lie around on the floor free for the picking, does not rain down on you from heaven. The fact that some people have found it come easy to them establishes no principle of investment success other than that luck happens. You cannot expect any metric of investment performance to point the way to easy wealth.

The basic difficulty is one with which quantum physicists are acquainted – the observer cannot separate himself from the observed. In a similar way, the investor cannot separate himself from the investment metric. By using it to help make his investment decision he changes what it shows him. The result at the level of the overall market after the decisions of millions of investors is that the metric says more about the observers than the observed.

I have no difficulty with this. The more this process is allowed to take place unhindered, the easier that making investments becomes for those with little experience of investment. The market itself makes the decision on what the fair price is at present for all that can be known to the market. The investor has still to take a view on the future and can be proved wrong or right on the future, but he has the right price for the now. I think it is a wonderful mechanism, one of social evolution's best.

But you still want to know what you have when you invest. You don't like to do it entirely blind. You still want to be one of those millions who use the tools of investment to make their choices. You also know that markets are not always efficient, that sometimes its process of price discovery does not proceed unhindered.

This is where the tools I have described come in. They all have a little to say about whether the prospects of the investment justify the price and they all touch on the theme of returns relative to the price. They give no complete answer, only hints, and mostly they confirm the justice of the price that the market has set.

Occasionally, however, they can help alert you to a pricing anomaly. Then you need to use them along with good judgement, common sense and an inclination to playing with numbers. Let's talk about that time share vacation home again.

What the promoter offers you is a price for a guaranteed use of the home free of other charges for two weeks a year. It is much less than you would pay if you bought the home outright and used it only two weeks a year, which is how much use many vacation homes are put to after the first few years of ownership.

Now pull out your calculator. Multiply your two-week price by 26 and you will have the equivalent of the full ownership price. I guarantee you that it is up two times what other nearby such properties would fetch. You then inquire how much other owners ask in rent for their two-week shares if they find they cannot go themselves. Multiply by 26 and calculate your cap rate. It will be very low.

And it is not an otherwise free-of-charge occupancy. There are hefty management, clean-up and insurance costs, even if just used two weeks a year.

What is more, you do not get a title deed. All you get is a claim against the company that owns the land and you do not know what other liabilities this company has incurred or is allowed to incur.

No, you say. You have used earnings, comparative prices, running costs and a little common sense about the security of the investment you have been pitched and you have come to a clear investment decision. Occasionally the tools of the trade will help show you the way.

But what really shows you the way is your own good judgement and this is not something you can pick up by applying tools from how-to books. Investment is like life itself, so dynamic, so infinitely varied in cause and effect that no investment story is exactly like any other. What is true for one can never be guaranteed true for another. The only rules that consistently apply are homilies like 'honesty is the best policy' or 'a stitch in time saves nine'. Good judgement is something that has a strong moral base and its roots in early life. It rewards cultivation and can open your eyes while others are still blinded. It is all about you, and this is just my basic message once again. You are your own best investment adviser.

CHAPTER 3

Government and . . .

. . . technology and innovation

In 1917 the Allied forces in the First World War received a new scout biplane, the Sopwith Camel, which quickly established dominance in the air over the Western Front. It was mostly made of wood and doped fabric with wires and wooden struts to hold its two wings in place while the torque from its rotary engine made it unstable in flight. It could fly little faster than 100 miles per hour and it carried only its pilot. It was still, however, considered an important advance in the relatively new technology of powered flight.

Shift forward fifty years and the big new commercial aircraft introduction of 1967 was the Boeing 737, in appearance a long white tube with an engine slung under each swept-back wing. It could fly at 500 miles per hour and it seated 120 people. Take that first Boeing 737 back fifty years in time travel, show it to the Sopwith Camel pilot and his jaw would drop to the ground.

But shift forward another fifty years from 1967 and the appearance of any standard commercial aircraft is a long white tube with an engine slung under each swept-back wing and a speed in the range of 500 miles per hour. Variants of the Boeing 737 still fly and are easily identifiable as such, though other aircraft have many times its passenger capacity. Show an example of any of them to a passenger from 1967 and he is likely to ask little more than, 'Do they still charge for drinks?' There would certainly be no dropping of jaws.

It happens that way in most technologies. Invention is followed by an explosion of development until the technology matures, development becomes little more than refinement and human ingenuity focuses on a different technology.

Curiously, however, it tends to be just about the time a technology matures that governments want to invest in advancing it. In aircraft technology it was notably the British and French governments that chose in the 1960s to pour a vast fortune into the development of a supersonic passenger aircraft as representing, in British Prime Minister Harold Wilson's words, 'the white heat of technology'.

In the event the Concorde was a rich man's indulgence for which there was never any real need or demand except among aerospace buffs. In Britain it proved, along with the earlier Brabazon and Comet, to be just another costly commercial aircraft failure needlessly inflicted on taxpayers. How much these misguided aerospace initiatives slowed the British economy, drained British creative spirit and hindered British advances in other technologies with a better future can never be known. Economic analysis cannot answer the question of what might have been. But the effect had to be considerable.

Consider another technology. In 1975 Intel founder Gordon Moore predicted that the number of integrated circuits on a computer chip would double every two years and for many years this Moore's Law proved surprisingly correct, resulting in an enormous digital revolution. Now, however, progressive miniaturisation is getting circuits closer to the size of the atom, one of the fundamentals of nature. The doubling has become ever more difficult, the explosive development stage is coming to an end. Nature's stop sign does not just prohibit. It prevents. The digital revolution has matured. Until the next breakthrough (quantum computing?) advance will now depend on refinement.

But, predictably, just as maturity sets in, governments across the world have decided to make the digital revolution the focus of massive public expenditure on innovation and technology. Every country, in China almost every city, has determined that it will become the new Silicon Valley. History repeats itself, but not how the politicians imagined. The Concorde was really no anomaly.

It should be no surprise. Consider what happens when a government makes such an intervention. The decision on exactly how to do it is given to a committee or number of committees after the politician has evoked the dream. The committee consists mostly of bureaucrats to stop the initiative from going awry but has an admixture of academics to give it intellectual standing plus some industry representatives who are naturally gung-ho boosters of any public expenditure on themselves.

Bureaucrats talk a lot about out-of-the-box thinking but the sad fact is that they are themselves rarely capable of it. Their task is to implement and monitor (two essential words of bureaucratese) the decisions of others. They work by rules and procedures. If they do not have them for any given contingency they draft them from reference to the closest approximation that they do have.

I see nothing wrong with this. It is exactly the right way for civil servants to do their normal jobs. The last thing their normal jobs require of them, however, is to nurture a revolution. Bureaucrats are inevitably led to favour yesterday's ideas when asked to recommend innovations.

Academics similarly are out of their depth. The sad fact is that the longer people stay in university the more unfit they render themselves for commerce. Yet the choice of what technologies people will find useful in the future is very much a matter of commerce.

Academics are all loud choristers of their universal theme song, *Gimme More Money*, when budget time rolls round but they have little experience of commercial disciplines, in particular of how much it hurts to suffer losses because of making bad choices with money. There is no P&L account in academia, no school of hard knocks, no bankruptcies, only the dean's displeasure.

Make that the abbot's displeasure and you have the university's antecedent, the monastery, where the brothers gathered to debate how many angels can stand on the point of a needle. Academics scorn this comparison, of course. Yet it is entirely apt in describing the natural tendencies of people who are subject to no hard tests of the value of their initiatives and who can evade the consequences of what they recommend to others.

Many worthwhile innovations have indeed received a helping hand from the public purse, mostly through the military, but public funding support for the dream of becoming 'the next Silicon Valley' is not driven by military requirements. It rather comes from politicians taking delight in hi-tech wonders and equating them with economic success. It is also a delusion. Success in hi-tech is critically dependent on owning intellectual property rights, which do not make as good a show as technicians dressed in lab coats and mouth masks observing the screen read-outs of fancy pieces of equipment in brightly lit clean rooms. Yet, it is the show that politicians and their committees buy. What they are not told is that the machinery is operated under licence, the products sold under someone else's brand name and the margins frighteningly thin. What they see is actually lo-tech applications of others' hi-tech ideas. They are not told this because the show is actually being held to prise concessions out of them for land, labour supply or tax.

Thus, beware. The market will long have priced in these considerations. It does so as keenly now with digital technology as it did with airlines and aircraft makers when aerospace was all the rage.

You need to be aware that it has done so, that seemingly attractive P/E ratios and earnings growth might not really be what they are touted to be when the ministry takes an interest. Beware of government booster talk parroted in the media and bear in mind the old principle that boring is best in investment. As a general guideline, where you hear talk of innovation stay out if government is moving in. As a specific guideline, bestow your favour at such times instead on the owner of the intellectual property rights.

. . . foreign investment

I have a counter-intuitive insight for you, the sort of thing which makes many people say, 'Go away. Where did you come up with that? It's obviously just plain wrong.'

Yet it is just plain right. My insight is that foreign investment does not give a country more investment.

Let us put this in the simple perspective of two countries, we shall say Sweden and Canada. A Swedish investor takes the view that his country's forest monoculture is distinctly inferior to Canada's forest diversity and that the future for the timber industry lies in the new world. He therefore decides to take seven million Swedish krona out of his accounts with Svenska Handelsbanken in Stockholm and invest it in Canadian forest industry stocks, for which he is warmly applauded by Canadian politicians.

But he trips up on the very first hurdle of this venture. Canadian forest industry stocks are denominated in Canadian dollars. The stockbroker handling the transaction for him in Canada will not accept payment in krona.

It is not a serious difficulty. The stockbroker refers our man to a branch of the Bank of Montreal just down the road, which takes his seven million krona and exchanges them for one million Canadian dollars. He now goes back to the stockbroker and buys the stocks he wanted.

And now the Bank of Montreal has a problem. What can it do with seven million krona in Canada where krona cannot as much as buy a sandwich for lunch. There is only one thing it can do. It maintains an account with Svenska Handelsbanken under a reciprocity agreement and it thus sends the krona right back to Stockholm.

Here now are two questions for you. One: By how much was the stock of investment capital in Sweden depleted by this investment? Two: By how much was stock of investment capital in Canada augmented?

You have it. The net loss to Sweden was zero and the net gain to Canada was also zero. Foreign investment brought Canada no more investment than it already had. All that happened was the ownership of seven million krona changed hands as did the ownership of one million Canadian dollars. In both cases the money actually stayed in the country from which it nominally came and the exchange made no difference to the totality of investment in either country.

It is an understanding that the minds of politicians and civil servants have difficulty grasping. They jump to grant citizenship in exchange for foreign investment, utterly convinced that they have made their country wealthier the easy way. All they have really done in many cases, however, is attract a shadier class of immigrant. People with money to hide find a multiplicity of passports convenient.

There are other advantages to this government mis-understanding of foreign investment. These mostly consist of easing your way to a worldwide reach for your portfolio and reducing some taxes imposed on your investment. Direct benefits are fewer. Keep your ears open for major shifts of policy and occasionally an opportunity will present itself. The more scatterbrained the politicians the more likely you are to find one.

. . . economic stimulus

Put a one hundred dollar banknote into one pocket. Now take it out and put it another. Has this made you richer?

The basic flaw in the reasoning for economic stimulus through government spending is that government looks at where the money goes but ignores where the money comes from.

The basic principle in play here is that you stimulate the economy every time you spend money. When you pay for groceries your money streams out many different ways and in each of these streams it turns the waterwheels of the economy. It helps pay the grocer, his suppliers, his staff, his shop rents, his utilities, his delivery vehicles and a very long list of others. All these people and industries are stimulated a little with every purchase you make.

It is the same with every investment you make. The difference with consumer purchase is that you yourself do not get anything immediately. Your return is deferred. But the construction workers of, let us say, a building in which you have invested are all paid and it stimulates their work.

Now assume that politicians think the economy is not growing quickly enough. We shall leave aside how much of this thought is likely to be presumption alone but let us say nine tenths of it. We shall also leave aside how they intend to spend the one billion dollars earmarked for their stimulus programme, but let us say mostly in innovation grants to small and medium enterprises. We shall leave all this aside, although it sorely needs commentary, because what we want to look at here is how the politicians intend to raise the one billion dollars for this stimulus.

First, we have the easy option. Let us tax the rich. I shall sign up for this wonderful idea without further demur if anyone can cite even one occasion on which it has been tried and has worked. Double the tax rates on the rich and, although you may get one sudden windfall of revenue, you will soon find your income from taxes on the rich cut by half instead. The rich will develop wings and fly abroad. You will probably also have to abolish the rule of law. It has far too much to say about property rights to make the rich an easy target for plunder. Additionally, you will soon discover that ostentatious spending on luxuries accounts for only a small proportion of what the rich do with their money. By far the largest bulk of it is invested. Take this from them and where you wished to stimulate investment you have actually stimulated disinvestment, a classic own goal.

The basic principle at work here is a simple one – the bottom stones always carry the greatest weight of the pyramid and the working poor always carry the greatest weight of taxation. However circuitous the route by which it comes to land on their shoulders, that is where it goes. It may be unfair but saying so has never changed things. Best then not load the weight on those shoulders in the first place. Taxing the rich is a placard waver's solution. It is an evasion of responsibility for the cost of public spending.

Next idea: we shall just tax everyone. It is certainly more practicable than taxing the rich alone but it is really just a variant of the idea that you can become richer by taking a banknote out of one pocket and putting it in another. If you take more money from people in tax and thus reduce their disposable income, they will have less to spend or invest and will therefore provide less stimulus to the economy. This will be matched by a greater stimulus in public spending but the gain in stimulus on the public side can never do more than offset the loss of stimulus on the private side. There can be no net gain. Economic stimulus through public spending is an illusion.

The most that can be said for it is that there may possibly be times when economic growth is slow because people are overly worried about the future. Sudden spending by government may then break them out of this pessimistic frame of mind. This kind of stimulus is called pump-priming and the number of times it is claimed to have succeeded is exactly matched by the number of times that no supporting evidence of this claim is advanced. How can anyone know that the majority of the population is too worried about the future? And if it later turns out that most people were right to be worried, which is much more likely, what politician has ever taken the blame for a mistimed stimulus that turned a subsequent mild recession into a severe one? This notion of pump-priming bespeaks an enormous conceit.

Government efforts at stimulus, however, are focused, which means that there will always be a few projects and enterprises that visibly succeed where they might otherwise have failed. A public relations army is then called out to make sure you know of the successes. What no-one can see is the extent of the very slight slowdowns suffered by hundreds of thousands of other enterprises from which stimulus has been drained. Yet the second must counter-balance all of the first.

Let us also dispense with the idea that if you instead borrow the money for a stimulus you can avoid burdening people with another tax. Once again, it does not work. It is still a case of taking a banknote from one pocket and putting it in another. The only difference is that with borrowing you tell people that you will pay the money back while with the tax you tell them that you will not. But you are still draining away money from them which leaves them with less disposable income to stimulate the economy on their own. It is still a zero-sum game.

The investment implications of all this to you are also zero sum. Do not let the announcement of a public stimulus campaign push you into making an investment that you might not otherwise make. Gamble, if you choose, that the announcement will push others to invest and that there is an opportunity here for a quick in-and-out speculative profit. But don't call it investment.

. . . jobs

Job creation, even more than quarterly economic data or the praise of journalists, is the yardstick by which politicians measure their performance.

In fact, however, government can no more create jobs than a gardener can create flowering plants. All that a gardener can do is ensure that his garden has the necessities of water, light, good soil and a pest-free environment so that the seed he sows can germinate, take root and grow into the plant he wants. But if he pushes his fingers into the soil to try pull the plant out from the seed all he will get is soiled fingers.

Likewise, when government ensures that the economy has such necessities as rule of law, a sound currency and an efficient infrastructure, the economy will itself produce jobs. But when government directly calls jobs into existence with a Genesis-like command of 'Let there be employment' it will just get the equivalent loss of employment elsewhere in the economy.

The money used to pay the wages of the new government-created jobs is taken from somewhere else in the economy where it would also have worked to create employment.

In fact, the picture for government-created jobs is worse than this. The best jobs, the ones that do the most to create widespread prosperity, are those involved in providing the goods and services that people most want at prices they can best afford. These are the kinds of jobs that the economy on its own brings into being when government restricts itself, gardener-like, to the necessary conditions for job creation. But when government creates jobs for the sake of creating jobs then these objectives of truly worthwhile jobs tend to go by the board.

Look at it from the perspective of the utterly absurd. Let us propose that we create jobs by digging a car tunnel all the way from the centre of your town to the middle of Antarctica. The jobs created this way would all be permanent jobs, they would all be related to the provision of infrastructure, a good thing, and, in order to create the maximum employment, we could specify that no tools more sophisticated than pick and shovel be allowed on the project. Lest there be any labour complaints we shall pay full union wages.

Absurd? Of course it is but any job that is created even partially in order to create a job rather than because some specific work needs to be done, shares to that degree in this absurdity. To the extent that there are better uses for the money, such jobs also undermine economic growth and inhibit further job creation.

Beware also of the term 'economic benefit' and the number of jobs that politicians claim to create through this form of hocus pocus. Economic benefit says that when you pay a worker one hundred dollars this person will create further jobs by spending the money and these further jobs will in turn create yet further jobs as the spending cascades through the economy. If you really squeeze the data hard you can create a multiplier effect of as much as ten times the original wages and the original number of jobs this way.

It is true; but what you are not told is that it is true for all forms of spending, whether it comes through jobs created by politicians or jobs that naturally arise through economic activity. There is no reason to think that the jobs which the politicians created have a higher multiplier effect. In fact, to the extent that they were not brought into being only to meet society's needs, they may have a lower multiplier effect.

They also tend to be a lower order of jobs. One of the most successful industry lobbies in any country is the tourism lobby. Tourism boosters all invoke economic benefits and make extravagant claims for the importance of tourism to the economy. They then further overstate it by ignoring that a great deal of tourist spending consists of shopping for imported goods and services. They ignore that the value of these imports is a deduction in calculations of gross domestic product.

But politicians generally accept the pitch uncritically and then devote a considerable share of public expenditure to tourist infrastructure, ignoring that tourism jobs are almost all low-paid menial ones. The workforce is thus further betrayed in the standard of the jobs available.

It is also betrayed when government uncritically accepts the demands of employers' lobbies that migrant labour be introduced to take up jobs that local workers scorn as paying too little. There is good reason for this scorn when a society has prospered so greatly that certain service jobs no longer make sense. Self-service fuel stops and self-operated lifts are the norm in developed countries. At prevailing wages there it just does not make sense to hire people to do what you can do yourself. Learning to do it yourself rather than rely on low-paid servants is one of the hallmarks of advanced societies.

It can be a wrenching change, however, and one way of putting it off is to bring in menial labour from abroad. Unfortunately, this is also a way of arresting social development and depressing the wages of local workers who are paid near the bottom of the income scale. The result is growing income polarity and a fertile field for social unrest, a government betrayal of its own working people.

. . . *moral hazard*

I do not actually like putting my savings at risk. I have to do it in my investment portfolio because there is no way I can avoid it and still put my money to work. But if I lose my money there all I can really do is kick the door (having no dog for a blame surrogate), say 'Ouch', feel stupid and leave it at that.

I would, however, be seriously annoyed to lose money on a bank deposit because that bank had mismanaged its assets and cannot pay back the full deposit. For an institution that bills itself on trust and usually pays less interest than the rate of inflation this would truly be adding insult to injury. Most people think this way and governments know it. They also recognise bank collapses as leading directly to the most dangerous financial crises.

Thus in most developed financial systems across the world we now have government-sponsored deposit insurance or straightforward deposit guarantees. If a bank goes bust the depositors will get all their money back up to a certain maximum, usually more than most people have on deposit. The national treasury stands behind this guarantee.

Unfortunately, the results of a deposit guarantee do not stop there. They have a direct effect on your thinking. There are any number of savings institutions covered by these guarantees and some may offer better rates than others or give you gifts if you put your money with them. Thus you shop around and pick the one that gives you the best deal. You no longer worry that they may get into financial trouble by being too aggressive. What value is their prudence to you when you hold a government guarantee that you will get your money back?

The guarantees also have an effect on the way that bankers think. They may previously have appealed to you on the basis of their prudence and their strong balance sheet but what value is this to the bank if the bank's customers no longer value it? The bank across the road is picking up new accounts by offering better air miles. The obvious solution to keeping the business is to tout as much in air miles through a 'special savers' package that also nudges up deposit rates. If it all goes wrong just direct the protests to the Ministry of Finance. It was the ministry that made the guarantees. The ministry will pay.

Things also go wrong on the other side of the bank balance sheet. Why worry so much that borrowers may not repay the advances made to them? It only happens to any worrisome degree in financial crises and these are intermittent and infrequent. In the meantime risky borrowers will pay much higher interest rates to find money. Not only will these higher rates allow the bank to offer more attractive deposit packages but most of the additional profit to be made this way can be paid out in higher salaries and bonuses to the bank's executives. If it all goes wrong the odds are that these executives will already have made their fortunes. There will not be much blame to throw around anyway. The depositors will not complain as long as they get their money back and the politicians will not want to make themselves look foolish for having made bad guarantees. If there are hearings of inquiry the bank can just confuse the issue with talk of market forces and let its lawyers hold off the tougher questions.

Sooner or later this progresses to a state in which most of the balance sheet is tied up not just in dubious loans and advances but in all sorts of toxic derivatives, and where the lion's share of the profits for years has been allocated to overpaid executives. The public no longer calls them bankers then. They are instead called 'banksters' and quite rightly so. The prudent banker has given way to the plundering financial gangster.

The same thing happens in the corporate headquarters suite. Executives who know their company inside out from having risen through its ranks from their first junior positions are now less in evidence. They have been replaced by headhunted financial wizards from outside the company. These people have learned how to take advantage of a false interest rate market through all the tricks of leveraged buy-outs, share buybacks and share option schemes. They also know how to reward themselves for their predatory ways and the result is that the gap between rich and poor widens even further.

But where did all the trouble start? You cannot separate the risk of investment from the investment itself, even for a bank deposit. The whole financial system goes awry when you do it, even for a bank deposit. It is called moral hazard and I have yet to see the government that recognises just how seriously it can undermine any economy.

A related problem arises when government attempts to alleviate the pain of bankruptcy. I am all in favour of limited liability. I would certainly hesitate to risk my money in any venture on which I could lose more than I put in. But there is nonetheless a price for the palliative of limited liability. It lies in forcing lenders to be more cautious in advancing money to corporations and in being quicker to call in their loans than they might otherwise have been. It becomes worse when bankruptcy under limited liability is further staved off by laws for debtor protection from creditors while court-mandated rescue attempts are staged. Mostly this only means that corporate losses are allowed to continue and creditors who could have retrieved their money instead see it drained away because they are not allowed to plug the leak. They naturally become even more risk averse with the result that the ups and downs of the economic cycle are accentuated. Financial crises are greater and come at more frequent intervals.

Risk is inseparable from investment. Remove it from in front of you and it will only come round and bite you from behind. Legislation cannot take risk away.

. . . where angels fear to tread
One of the biggest failures of government intervention in many years has been in the surrender by politicians to academics of responsibility in monetary matters. It is a mistake that could not be made until about fifty years ago and then became the norm. It has consequences beyond what most people recognise.

The story is easily told in outline. In the 1970s the world finally went off the gold standard. Until then, should any country run a deficit in trade with the rest of the world, a deficit not made up by foreign investment, the level of the gold in its vaults would dwindle and the country would be forced to raise interest rates to attract money back. The value of the gold standard, in other words, lay not in the gold but in the standard, in a discipline that it enforced on the monetary authorities of all countries that adhered to the standard.

Gone and departed now and not hugely mourned, except by gold bugs, as it could probably not have survived anyway in today's world. But the point is that there was nothing to replace the gold standard except trust in the monetary authorities of the countries that abandoned it, and within twenty years this began to prove a misplaced trust, first in the United States, then in other countries.

What happened is that the politicians said, 'Jeez, I don't understand all this stuff. I never did it in college. Maybe we should just call in the experts.'

And they called in the academics. These experts forthwith came up from their remote monastic cells, gowned in academic solemnity, chanting their Keynesian mantra of aggregate demand economics. What they prescribed was first a reduction of interest rates through discount rate manipulation and then central bank purchases of government bonds until a state of full employment and two per cent inflation had been attained. This wonderful elixir, said these magicians, would inevitably cure all the economy's ailments if consumed exactly as prescribed.

And when it did not work as prescribed, they just prescribed more of it, right through a financial crisis of their making, and then yet more of it right through another and greater financial crisis of their making and, even then, yet more of it. All the while, the politicians allowed them to do it.

The result was that they destroyed the price of money.

Yes, money has a price. It is the price you pay to use other people's money or the price they pay to use yours. There are many different terms for it, some of which I have described in the previous chapter. We shall call it interest rates. What the academics who took over the US Federal Reserve Board did by artificially lowering interest rates through their machinations was to distort the process through which the market prices all the different investment proposals put to it.

The first consequence was an enormous speculative boom in stock and bond prices. If the prevailing earnings yield of an economy is 6 per cent, let us say, and you artificially reduce it to 3 per cent, then for any given level of earnings you double the price of the asset that generates these earnings.

In simpler terms, take a stock trading at $100 a share with earnings per share of $6. This stock is thus trading at a price-to-earnings multiple of 16.6x or, expressed alternatively, at an earnings yield of 6 per cent. For our purposes we shall say this is an average stock of average earnings growth and earnings quality. Investors thus price it at the average P/E, or earnings yield, of the entire market, which in turn rests on the average risk-free rate of return for the entire economy.

Now along comes the central bank and, through magic conceived in academia, artificially depresses the economy's risk-free rate of return to virtually zero. This has the result of pulling down the average earnings yield of the market from 6 per cent to, let us say, 3 per cent. The stock still generates earnings of $6 a share but we now price these earnings on the basis of a 3 per cent earnings yield, a price-to-earnings multiple of 33x. The result is that the share price jumps from $100 to $200, with no change in profitability, a straight gift to speculators from the central bank. It does not usually work quite as quickly and simply as this but it is nonetheless the clear trend of events.

Much the same happens in the bond market, where the effect is more direct because it is through massive bond purchases, with the consequent rising prices for bonds, that the central bank drags interest rates down. There is the added effect in the bond market that the process encourages leveraged buy-outs. In this game, speculator gangs issue low-yielding bonds to buy out the share capital of listed companies. They can then use part of the company cash flow to pay the interest on the bonds. Why work for a living when money grows on trees?

In real estate the rising home prices encourage home-owners to take out at least a portion of their paper gains in hard cash by re-mortgaging their homes. The cash then flows to a big box store for such toys as pressure cleaners, new laptops and power tools to make the back porch a barbecue deck. From the big box store the money flows to the producers in China of these things. The result is a growing trade deficit that the politicians then blame on China instead of on themselves for allowing academics to toy with things they don't understand.

And the weight of all this falls heaviest once again on the backs of the working poor. They find that even the meagre savings they can put by no longer give them any returns to help ameliorate their living circumstances and, in fact, dwindle steadily in value in line with inflation.

The cost is paid elsewhere as well. When the link between share price and earnings is severely weakened corporations can engage in enterprises to which the doors would earlier have been shut by market earnings discipline. They can then sweep aside rivals who still think earnings matter. Most of the big winners of the US stock market after the 2008 financial crisis fall into this category and it has weakened the US economy. Should the new earnings paradigm eventually falter, both conquering giants and vanquished midgets will go with it.

Similarly, in the bond market leveraged buy-outs have become so aggressive that once-energetic corporations have become sapped of all their strength through the amount of LBO debt they carry. They then struggle along as what are called 'debt zombies' in fear that any rise in interest rates will put an end to them. It amounts to just more weakening of the economy.

This was not intended of course. The idea was that low interest rates would stimulate general economic activity with the result that the economy would soon operate at its full potential and all jobseekers would find good jobs.

But it simply has not happened. The speculation in financial asset prices has choked off the supply of credit to the Main Street economy. That supply could never have amounted to much in any case as this particular form of academic magic did not seek to encourage Main Street with a greater supply of money, but only with a lower price for it. In the event Wall Street took what money was available. Main Street did not want it anyway as it did not think commercial conditions really warranted more borrowing. Sadly, even as this outcome was becoming apparent, Europe and Japan chose to ape the US academic magic with even greater fervour.

In an extremity of arrogance, the entire world was made an experimental test bed for novel academic theories that were, from the beginning, detached from reality and never proven anywhere except theoretically in academic journals where the only failure is the failure to publish.

But it was first of all a government failure in scorning bankers to appoint academics instead to the crucial role in the underpinnings of finance.

The result for investors has been to accentuate the volatility of financial markets while rendering invalid the traditional benchmarks of investment value. At a deeper level it threatens a long-held social compact that people who save their money can, through investment, join the captains of industry in their economy's growth. I see no good in this anywhere.

. . . *social spending*

Pick a public transport infrastructure project, any such project, be it roadway, bridge, airport, railway or any such like. Eeenie, meenie, miny moe, okay, railway it is, and for our purposes we shall make this a high-speed railway built at public expense between two cities. It will be good for business, say the bureaucrats, good for social cohesion, it will bring jobs and it will boost the economy.

We shall also assume, just as water is wet and the sun rises in the east, that this railway has not a hope of turning a profit for the public purse. Even on an EBITDA weasel valuation that pretends that major costs do not exist, it will still operate in the red for any level of passenger fares that the public can be persuaded to pay.

But, say the bureaucrats, what does this matter? This is a social project undertaken for social purposes, for the good of all members of society. Why do you expect us to value such a project in money terms as if it were a commercial venture? Not everything can be assessed in terms of dollars and cents, you know. Some things have a value beyond money. Can money buy you love?

Well, yes, it can, say I, and mostly does because that is the way evolution has coiled our genes. But this is not the fight I want to pick here. The one I am looking for comes from a simple question: How do you measure the social benefits that make the railway worth building if it is wrong to value it in commercial terms?

I assume here that the value of social benefits is not infinite. There must be a level at which we agree that the social benefit of any given project is not worth the cost. If this is not so then I shall go back to my long-tunnel argument. In this case I propose building three undersea railway tunnels from New York to the town of Le Havre in France. They would connect Europe and America more closely, build social cohesion, create lots of jobs, encourage trade and some people might appreciate being able to take the train all the way instead of having to fly. Perhaps we should make it five tunnels to cater for future demand. The project would produce at least some degree of social benefit and if we are to say that the value of any social benefit is infinite then this is certainly a worthwhile project, whatever the cost.

Right then, so we agree that this would actually be a ridiculous project for the money it would cost, that the value of any social benefit is not infinite and that we need to know of any social benefit whether it is worth the effort of bringing it into being. How then do we measure the value of social benefit to determine whether any project of social benefit is actually worth its cost?

This question has never been answered, has in fact, to my knowledge, never even been properly asked by people who invoke social benefit to justify public expense.

Do not ask me to answer it. If we are not to pose the question in money terms then I think it impossible to answer. All I can suggest is that we do things the other way round for a change. Instead of having the public purse put up the money and the beneficiaries pay for it with warm feelings of appreciation, I propose that we have the public purse contribute the warm feelings and the beneficiaries put up the money.

But let us pose the question in money terms and see if we can define the social benefits that way. We shall start with the notion that our high-speed railway is good for business because businessmen can travel more quickly between their businesses in the two cities this way and, as everyone knows, time is money in business.

This is certainly talking my line. I am the one who stresses the importance of interest rates, which are all about time and money. The difference, however, is that with interest rates we are talking of defined percentages or amounts of money over a defined span of time, say 10 per cent per year. These are hard figures. Where now are the hard figures on how much money the businessman saves by a journey time of one hour less than the journey previously took?

Yes, scratch your head again. There is only one way to answer this question and it is to ask this businessman himself. How much more is he willing to pay for this journey than he previously paid for the slow chug-chug train? Would it be $100, $50 or $20?

Let's say he comes back with a figure of $20. We then go to the accountant to ask what the break-even fare for the trip would be, assuming a reasonably full train and taking proper account of all costs (no EBITDA, please). The accountant runs his fingers over his calculator, looks up and tells us that his best estimate is $80.

We now have our answer. The social benefit of this railway to the businessmen is not worth the cost of building it. He has set a figure on this benefit, he is the most suitable person to do it, and he has told us as directly as he can that its social value to him does not come up to our mark. Why then should we build the railway at all?

We can, in fact, carry out this exercise, for all of our railway's passengers and for all the merchants handling all the goods that might be carried on it. Are they willing to pay the cost of a faster journey time? If yes then the social benefit to them outweighs the cost, if no then it does not. The best judges of the matter can all offer their opinion of the social value. No better way of doing so exists than just asking them.

So here is the truth of the matter. In projects involving the expenditure of money the only valid way of quantifying social value is exactly the same as the only way of quantifying commercial value. There is no difference between the two.

This does not mean that the answer in every case must come from the end user. The question of whether to build a hospital will still be decided by the Ministry of Health rather than by the patients when it is the ministry that pays. But it can still be quantified in this unified social/commercial way. Call in the accountants and work out an approximate break-even cost for any standard procedure. Does the ministry think this worthwhile? Then it will pay. Does the ministry think it excessive? Then it must make a hard choice between the social value that this medical procedure brings as against the social value that some other use of the money may bring. It's a tough choice but it can at least be quantified and this is at least better than completely ignoring the cost of social benefits, which is what most people do when invoking social value.

It is not a universal solution to the problem. I cannot imagine trying to establish the appropriate levels of social welfare payments by quantifying their social value. If I were to say that we should pay recipients $1 million each you will say, 'Don't be silly.' If I were to say that we should pay them $1 each you will also say, 'Don't be silly.' Somewhere in between these two figures lies the most appropriate amount and I am as baffled as anyone else about what exactly it should be. My system of quantifying social value breaks down here.

But it covers enough to supply a sorely needed discipline for a great deal of government expenditure.

And here is the general lesson of it for you. When governments are so kind as to offer you the wonderful opportunity of buying shares in an infrastructure project built for the unquantified social benefits, you say, 'Thank you ever so much but all my money is tied up in bubble gum just now.'

Of course, if you see hard evidence that they have mispriced the initial offering (it happens more often than you might think) then dive in for a quick speculative bet. But jump right out again soon afterwards. It is a speculation, not an investment.

CHAPTER 4

Markets and the law

The protocols of dealing

Buying and selling in financial markets is crucially different from buying and selling in a shopping mall. In the mall the buyers are distinct from the sellers. You are either one or the other and there is no difficulty in telling which you are. In financial markets, however, anyone can be either buyer or seller and can switch between the two instantly.

There is also no such thing as a price tag. The price has to be worked out between buyer and seller on each occasion that they deal with each other. And while in the mall people buy only small amounts of whatever it is they want, in financial markets they can buy and sell either small amounts or many tens of millions of dollars' worth at any one time. Neither buyer nor seller, however, will immediately say in what size they wish to deal. There have thus to be some protocols on how they approach each other.

In financial markets a typical protocol if you want to buy X is to ask your intended counterparty, 'Are you making a market in X?' You do not say either 'I want to buy' or 'I want to sell.' You give no hint of your intention other than that you want to deal. Your counterparty then says something like, 'Yes, nine twenty, nine thirty.' This bid/offer quotation means that your counterparty is willing to buy X from you at price of $9.20 or sell X to you at a price of $9.30.

Note that your counterparty still does not know whether you are buying or selling and that you do not want him to know yet. If you told him that you are a buyer, not a seller, he may make that offer price $9.40 instead of $9.30.

But he also does not want to quote too wide a spread between his bid and offer because then you will just go to someone else. If raising his offer price to $9.40 also makes him raise his bid price from $9.20 to $9.30, you might just hit this bid at $9.30 and it will be *he* who pays ten cents more than he is really prepared to pay. By not telling him you keep him honest.

We shall assume you like his bid/offer. You then say something like, 'I lift your offer of $9.30 for 10,000 units.' Of course, if it is rather ten million units you want to buy you may also want to ask him first in what size he is dealing. This is valuable information as it may tell you what direction the price of X is likely to move that day. You will therefore only do it if you yourself truly are dealing in size. He has to trust you then that you are a serious buyer and not just trying to get market information. But the professional dealers know each other and this level of trust between them is rarely betrayed.

Now let's shift to a specific financial market, the London interbank market for US dollars. This was a sizeable market because US dollars are heavily used for trade and investment round the world. Banks that participate in this market constantly find themselves with more demand than they have US dollars available or more supply than they have demand. Through the interbank market they can keep their requirements in balance for a range of different maturities, one night, for instance, or perhaps three months.

This market also works on a bid/offer basis, but for interest rate rather than for a dollar figure, and the key rate for many people used to be the London interbank offered rate, LIBOR (it will be phased out by 2021). Thus a US dollar three-month LIBOR of four per cent meant that a participant in the market was offering to lend US dollars at an annualised interest rate of four per cent to other participants in the market for a period of three months.

The reason this was a key rate is that LIBOR was used round the world as a benchmark for other much bigger loans. The agreements on these loans would typically say that the interest to be charged on them would be something like one quarter or one tenth of a per cent higher than, let us say, six-month LIBOR. This not only allowed lenders and borrowers to come to practicable agreements on how interest rates would be assessed for longer-term loans but allowed lenders to raise the money from the London interbank market at a low risk although a slim profit. The LIBOR rates used for these purposes were calculated daily as an average of what a number of market participants offer.

All well and good, but now we come to the problem highlighted by a scenario in which one of the people who calculate the official LIBOR rates calls a market maker in this interbank market and asks, 'What are you quoting for three-month LIBOR?'

It is an improper question. The market maker is not being asked for his bid/offer but only for his offer. No genuine participant in the market would do such a thing. It is an invitation to being given a false offer. Obviously, this caller is either a fool who will soon lose all his money or, more likely, someone who does not really wish to deal but only wants information for free.

Let me stress this last point. A firm LIBOR quote was valuable information. The precise interest rate charged on hundreds of billions of dollars of lending around the world depended on it. You do not get valuable information for free in financial markets. You pay for it by dealing, by asking a market maker for a bid/offer and then actually hitting that bid or lifting that offer for at least a small sum of money so that you can be sure the market maker has given you an honest bid/offer.

I remember watching it classically done years ago in the Tokyo dealing room of a big American investment bank for which I worked for a number of years. It was a day of listless market movement and the head trader felt he had temporarily lost the pulse of the market. He stood up at his desk, loudly called out that he was a buyer of a bellwether market derivative and his sales staff promptly worked their phones to scour the market for offers. A few minutes later he stood up again and said he was a seller of the same derivative. Once again the sales staff worked their phones. The responses, first one way, then the other, told the head trader what he wanted to know about the general market movement. He had paid for the information he wanted.

There is also a famous story, probably apocryphal, of how the Great Bear of Wall Street, Jesse Livermore, had a market spy run into his office one day and shout out, 'Jesse, the Syndicate is selling Sugars!'

Livermore said nothing in reply but stood up to inspect the ticker tape and then told his dealer, 'Buy me two thousand Sugars.'

'Jesse, Jesse, they're selling, not buying. You'll lose your shirt,' the spy protested.

Again, Livermore said nothing but told his dealer, 'Buy me another two thousand.'

'Jesse, no, they're selling!' his spy called out.

Livermore only kept two eyes on the ticker tape and two ears cocked at his dealer. Eventually he said, 'That went pretty fast. Sell two hundred thousand.'

He had confirmed his spy's story in the only sure way he knew of doing it.

So what is our market maker in the London interbank market to say when someone calls to ask him for his three-month US dollar offer rate? It is first of all an insult to him to imply that he makes his markets in so unprofessional a manner. More than that, it is a waste of his time. His department of his bank critically depends on him for its results, he cannot afford mistakes in his trading and he is keyed up, absorbed in the market's movement. But now some tosser who will never deal anyway wants a free one-way quote.

The market maker is free to tell such a caller anything he wants. He has no obligations to this person. He therefore cites a figure that is skewed to the way he wants the market perceived that day but is still close enough to the market to be credible to people who do not know. To my way of thinking it is exactly the right way to deal with people who toy with the market.

But the law says it is a crime and some years back several banks paid big fines because their market makers did it. One man even went to prison.

I say this was a grave miscarriage of justice.

Inside information

Picture yourself scouring the market for something worthwhile and finding your attention increasingly drawn to stock X. Let me wait a day or two and think this over, you tell yourself, and if I still like it at that time I shall buy it.

The very next day, however, the share price leaps upwards, right from the opening bell, and continues rising. Three days later all is revealed. The company has just signed a big contract that will guarantee earnings for years into the future. The insiders knew it would be signed a few days earlier and jumped into the market immediately, which is why price went up ahead of the announcement. You naturally feel aggrieved. 'I could have been in on that one,' you say, 'but I was cheated by the insiders. It's not a level playing field.'

Now let's imagine the same you in a different place. This time you are a holder of the stock and you are thinking of selling it. But once again you decide to wait a day or two and give yourself a little time to think it over.

The very next day, however, just as in the first scenario, the share price leaps upwards on the market right from the opening bell and continues rising. But this time when you learn why it happened, you blow out a sigh of relief and bless your luck. You might have sold just before the price jump but you didn't and, because the insiders then started buying, you participated in the rally. Do you then say, 'Thank you, Mr Insider, for doing me a good turn?'

Now let us set these two scenarios in reverse and try our fortunes once again with you as a holder of the stock in the first scenario. This time the share price suddenly drops just before you yourself are about to sell and you find out three days later that it happened because the insiders learned that the company was about to lose a big contract. 'Damn insider crooks,' you say. 'I could have sold in time but they got in the way.'

Now, however, let's imagine that you intend to be a buyer of the stock but you hold off for that one day and then decide not to buy at all when the price plunges on that day. First you must find out why this untoward movement occurred. When you do find out, you say, 'Whew, my lucky stars saved me this time. I could have been landed with a dog of a stock.' But do you also then say, 'Thank you, Mr Insider, for doing me a good turn?'

No, you do not. And you do not need to. The insiders did it all for themselves with no thought for you. You need spare them no thought. Yet, you could easily have been either buyer or seller, both times, in both scenarios, and people like you, total outsiders, were undoubtedly in these positions in all cases.

So here is the big question: What then was the net loss or net gain to the universe of outsiders from having insiders jump in before them?

Answer: Not much. A few insiders profited or avoided loss on a few shares when members of the general investing public might have done so. But their period of opportunity was only brief before their activities drove the share price to the right level for the news of which they had advance knowledge. Unless the whole company was corrupt right to the entire board of directors, they also risked their jobs and reputations if they were caught.

Meanwhile, all other shareholders were not affected in the slightest, the company's operations suffered no ill effects and some other investors actually had reason to be glad that the share price made an early move. It's an ill wind that blows nobody good.

I fully understand the indignation about insider dealing. These insiders are already paid their salaries, bonuses and share options, paid well. They have no right to stick their hands into the pot this way, too.

If this moral objection is your only one, however, then I think you do best to take it up with the vicar. Our purpose here is rather to discover whether it disrupts the workings of the market or is corrosive of the social order. Only then is there reason to call in the law.

Regulators will argue there is such reason. The investing public will not participate in a financial market that it perceives is dominated by insiders, they say. In order to keep financial markets healthy, we must keep the insider dealing out.

It appears a reasonable assertion but I personally never have seen clear evidence of it, no strong inverse correlation between public participation in a financial market and the degree of insider dealing in that market, no indication that fear of insider dealing stops companies from raising new money on a market. There should be but there is not. Markets just do not operate by the moral code that regulators might like to impose on them.

One reason for this is the one I have just pointed out. For every market movement, whatever the cause, there are as many people who win along with the insiders as there are more shares in the company than the insiders have bought or sold. The outsiders are never hurt quite so badly as regulators would have you believe.

And in one way they always benefit. Insider dealing gets you rapid price discovery. In other words, the share price moves more quickly to reflect all the knowable influences on it. This means that your odds on whether you will win or lose with any stock are brought more quickly to that

50/50 balance which gives you the fairest possible deal on any investment you wish to make.

We cannot prevent all insider dealing anyway. Corporate directors and executives are routinely forbidden from dealing in the shares of their company for a period of weeks before quarterly earnings announcements. This is to prevent them from taking advantage of anything that the results may reveal. But it is a rare corporate executive who does not have an instinctive knowledge of the trend of events all year long. Are we then to ban all directors and executives from any dealing at any time? What are we to say then to the founders of successful companies who want to divest themselves of some of their shareholdings on the reasoning of not holding all their eggs in one basket?

I do not say I approve of insider dealing. I share the moral indignation most people feel about it. I only say that in practice it is nowhere near as damaging to the operation of financial markets as regulators claim it to be.

In any case you have one good way of staving off the depredations of insiders on your personal portfolio. Don't deal so often. Pick your stocks and stick with them. The insiders cannot touch you if you don't deal.

Market manipulation

I am not much of a poker player. I cannot keep a straight face. If I am dealt a good set of cards my body language will show it immediately. And I simply cannot bluff. The art of it is beyond me. Others always know. From this you may be sure that if I am ever accused of market manipulation I am not guilty.

To manipulate prices on a financial market you must do one or both of two things. You must convince other participants in the market that you are a very big buyer/seller and they will be crushed if they do not get out of your way; or you must start a believable rumour that some very good/bad news is about to come the way of your manipulation target. There is not really much else you can do. You must, in other words, be a good poker player.

It helps, of course, if you are very rich. People can then be more easily led to think you are going to move the market. This can work two ways, however. People are then also likely to think it of you any time that you enter the market and you will generally find prices moving away from you whenever you deal. You will then have to be more secretive when dealing.

I am talking mostly of Asia as it is where my experience lies. I cannot really speak for America or Europe. But in Asia, at least, some big tycoons can be quite compulsive about their market activity. They have been dealing all their lives and they just cannot stop. I asked a friend of mine once why the big property development company for which he worked was so convoluted that every project on which it embarked was a subsidiary of another subsidiary three levels removed from the holding company.

'Oh, it's the old man,' my friend replied. 'He calls his son up every morning and asks how much money he can have to play the market today. We can tell him truthfully there isn't much because it's all tied up in different accounts and we can't pool it together that quickly. It's the only way to stop him.'

Sometimes the tycoons do it for reasons other than immediate profit. One boss for whom I worked maintained a small listed family company to which he felt a duty of parental care. As he saw things, no father would throw a tender young infant out on the street and say, 'There you go, kid. It's a tough world. Hope it works for you.'

No, that just would not do. Proper care and duty required that twice a year he would run this thinly traded stock up and down again in seemingly heavy trading over a few days so that all holders who wanted out could get out and others could get in again if they chose. Occasionally he would reward one or two people on the dealing desk with a better bonus than others got by telling them when to get in and out of the stock. This, however, was many years ago. The law now demands, alas, that people trapped in a thinly traded stock must stay there.

In my experience it is actually the not-so-rich who are most likely to try to turn a quick profit by manipulation. A common ploy is to work as a twosome picking on something small and thinly traded. The two then throw it back and forth between each other, lifting the price gradually in heavier than normal trading volumes to give the illusion of sudden wider interest. If they are successful in attracting others they may start moving the price more aggressively until they are ready to make their big move and dump a large amount of stock on the duped buyers at a high price.

But they had best beware the pitfall and the ambush. The pitfall is that the algorithms in the digital brains tracking the market down in the offices of the securities commission may spot them. Then there will be regulatory trouble. The ambush is laid by the professional dealers on the market who have a keen nose for this sort of game and know how to make their own big move just before the would-be manipulators do it, thus lumbering them with more stock than they had when they started and at a lower price on the market. It is my guess that more money is generally lost than made in this kind of manipulation.

The regulators do not interfere much, however, with the manipulations of the big investment banks. A traditional game, spawned in New York by these princes of the market, is called the 'greenshoe'. When bringing a new stock to the market they secure the right to issue about 15 per cent more stock than originally planned if there is big demand for the first 30 days of trading. Should this big demand indeed materialise and the price rise in the initial trading, they sell the stock short at the higher price and then demand the 15 per cent from the company at the lower issue price. If the price instead goes down they pick up the stock at the lower market price and then sell it to committed buyers to whom they have shorted it at the higher issue price. It is a game of heads-I-win-tails-you-lose and it is straight market manipulation. But the regulators will not touch them. Regulation is about fishing for minnows.

Rumour-mongering is another way of trying to manipulate a market but a more difficult one. The problem is that the professionals in the market know instinctively what has the ring of truth and what does not. False rumours rarely last long and have little effect. Rumours that persist invariably have at least a core of truth. It is just one of the ironies of the market that the lies are mostly to be found in official statements to the stock exchange while the much maligned rumours are mostly true.

In the end the truth about market manipulation is a version of the aphorism, attributed (unreliably) to Abraham Lincoln, restated: You can cheat some of the people all of the time and all of the people some of the time but you cannot cheat all of the people all of the time. My evidence for it is the unrestrained workings of the United States stock market in the years after Lincoln's death. There was very little law to get in the way of such accomplished robber barons as Jay Gould, Jim Fisk and Daniel Drew but over the career extent of their manipulations the record indicates that they actually lost money. The market itself disciplined them. Healthy financial markets have a way of doing that. They may concentrate wealth in the formative stages of any new industry, as they did for the railway ventures of Gould, Fisk and Drew but in settled industries they do not tolerate cheats for long and then they do more to reduce than increase wealth disparity.

Do not confuse manipulators, however, with that other evildoer of the market, the speculator. All manipulators are speculators but not all speculators are manipulators. Have you yourself, for instance, ever bought an investment not because you valued its dividend/coupon and not because you thought it a good way to preserve your savings but because you expected the price to go up and give you a trading profit? You are not an investor then. You are a shifty-eyed, greasy-haired speculator. Let us just be glad that you are not also a manipulator.

Speculators are most excoriated when markets crash. They are then invariably blamed for the crash and despised for having made money from it. I take the opposite view. Vultures do not feed on live meat and speculators do not feed on healthy markets. When they are actively taking short positions on a market, hindsight almost always shows that this market had been artificially supported, commonly through government agencies, and is naturally weak. Speculators then do the entire investment community a service by taking the market down before the rot spreads further. Speculators act as a market's clean-up service in the same way that vultures act as Nature's. They are not a pretty sight at such times but there would be worse to see without them. They look better when they pick a market up from its bottom and are esteemed for their courage and astute investment insight.

Either way, you are proof against them and against manipulators if you take the same remedial approach that I recommend against insider dealers. Don't deal so often. You will rarely be ahead of the market anyway. Pick your investment and stick with it.

Front running

Front running is the sneak's way of making money. It is
easily done, easily caught, and rarely makes the perpetrator
any serious money in any one act of it. It is at the low end
of the larceny scale in financial crime. Front runners are
the pickpockets of the market.

One variant of it, however, I always thought a classic of
sophistication. This was in the early days of my career as
an investment analyst when the Hong Kong stock market
had only recently been celebrated in London as the coming
thing, which indeed it was. For a period it was actually the
London interest that drove the market, mostly through a
small number of London fund managers and the London
branches of a small number of Hong Kong stockbrokers.
The market drew such attention that a notable London
bookmaker started making a book on daily Hang Seng
Index closes.

A small cabal of the key fund managers and brokers then
joined heads every day, compared their order books and
appointed one of their number in turn to make the bet
with the bookmaker. They cleaned him out of the game
within a matter of weeks. Tell me, how is laughter defined?

The sneak's practice is often as much a case of after-running
as front-running or, at least, used to be so. Instead of
jumping in the market before a client's order raises the
price, for instance, he keeps all his completed dealing slips
on his desk with no entry for the account to which the
stock will go or from which it will come. Only after
exchange hours does he decide who will get what, along

with the routine 'one for me' allocations. The most notable practitioner I knew of this form of 'retro-booking' eventually lost his job when he never dealt his boss in. Very silly. The boss did not so much object to pickpocketing as to being excluded from the take. The firm never did well. The market grew wise to both dealer and boss.

This was in the old days of paper contract notes and settlement by physical exchange of share certificates. It was supposedly put a stop to even in those days by a requirement that all dealing rooms recognised by the exchange must have a tamper-proof stamping machine to stamp the time and date of the transaction on all dealing slips. Machines break down, however, and thus a key had to be made available in each office for repairs. How interesting then that in at least one dealing room of which I knew the chief dealer wore this key from a chain around his neck.

Old days, I say, but new days too. The pickpocketing continues, only now it is the digits of an algorithm rather than the digits of a hand which do it. Flash trading, one notable American writer on investments called it. The front runner reaches the virtual exchange a split nanosecond before the order arrives and transacts the business at a slightly disadvantageous price to the client. Make your link fast enough and you can make a lot of money. Although this game has probably changed now that it has been spotted, pickpockets don't go away just because they have been seen.

But you have to wonder how some people think they can actually make a safe career practice of it. If I have not yet said it for the hundredth time, let me do so now. The market knows, it just knows. The combined awareness of millions of participants cannot be fooled for long. Yes, some people make themselves rich. Many more do not. And markets exact a toll on people tarred with front running. Their careers go downhill and then you see them on the street years later, their faces worn, their suits sagging on them. They say they are fine but, if they are not reduced to peddling life insurance to old acquaintances, they try to sign you up for an account with an unknown bottom-fishing brokerage. You pity them and you say, 'Yeah, okay, send me the account forms' but you never fill them in. No regulator could ever reduce people quite so far.

And, once again, you yourself have an absolutely first-class defence against front-running. Don't deal so often.

The regulators

I am a big believer in evolution, particularly social evolution. There is nothing quite like a market to show you how quickly natural selection can find what really works and give it the resources to make it work. There is nothing quite like a market to take the stuffing out of ideas that do not work, despite all the loud claims by their backers of imminent great success, and to let you see later just why it was all nonsense.

Social evolution also works in other ways on human institutions. No matter the reason for which they are founded, their purpose sooner or later also becomes their own grandeur and preservation. It is not intended. It just happens because it is the way natural selection works. Those institutions grow and survive which set the greatest store by growth and survival. Within them the people who prioritise growth and survival are the ones who most often rise to manage them.

It is not enough to keep them thriving when their survival also depends on how much a market values them. Then they must see first to the purposes for which they are formed and to the direct support of the public. Then their grandeur and survival are subject to nature's requirement that they also be the fittest in what they do.

But if they do not operate within a market, if they rather survive at the whim of government, then they can become very large indeed and survive for a long time while at the same time providing little of benefit to the public. I do not say that securities regulators are as bad this way as the Ministry of Administrative Affairs (or the military) but they are certainly empire builders who overstate their value to the investing public and underestimate the burden they impose.

At their worst, they can be very nasty. A common practice in the United States, for instance, when regulators have a suspected offender in their clutches is to try to spread the guilt as wide and high as they can. They will threaten the directors of his or her company with criminal charges which, even if the directors could reasonably refute in court, will cost them their reputations, years of their time and millions of dollars in legal fees.

The regulators then promise that they will 'ringfence' their victims out of any legal proceedings if their company will agree to pay a substantial fine and if neither it nor the directors will protest the regulators' allegations of guilt. Inevitably, the victims of this blackmail accede to it. Who wants the alternative of all that grief?

The regulators then call a press conference, present the public with the scalp of this big fine and say, 'We caught us another evildoer.' The public applauds and the chief regulator forthwith steps on the first rung of the ladder to a political career.

Meanwhile, the most that the company and its directors can say in response is, 'No comment.' Anything more will result in the 'ringfence' being unfenced. Bear it in mind when next you read or hear an account of a serious corporate financial crime for which a big fine was paid but no trial ever held, no defence ever heard, no conviction registered and no jail sentence imposed. Guilty?

At their best, regulators do you a good service of fore-stalling theft by intermediaries of the market. Let your investment adviser 'confuse' your account with his own personal one, use balances you maintain with him without your permission or not keep up the minimum amount of capital required of him and the regulators will be all over him. I applaud. Good job.

But how big an empire can you build on just one minor aspect of police work? If you are to be a big tough regulator who catches everyone's attention when you swagger through Dodge City you need big crimes against which you can be the public's first line of defence. It helps if you can also make them appear more heinous. You may even need to make them up if others will not do it for you. Just what, for instance, does the term 'rat trading' mean? It must be bad, I know. It involves the word 'rat'. But I have never been able to pin down a single definition.

The burden of it all is much greater than just the swiftly rising annual budget of the local securities commission. Every stockbroker, private banker, fund manager and listing sponsor, every firm that has anything to do with investment must also maintain a growing compliance department filled with hosts of the righteous, all well paid, all granted full benefits at civil-service standards and all eager to do battle with the forces of evil.

The curious thing, however, is how little they know about the forces of evil. They are mostly lawyers, a large number of them unsuccessful in private practice, just past the trainee stage or not quite officially qualified, and they have very little experience of investment.

It would not be so bad if law and investment were kin pursuits but they are not. The subtleties of how markets work are largely foreign to a profession steeped in hard and fast rules. The result is that the 'kids', which is how I cannot avoid thinking of so many of them, quickly impute a criminal association to anything they do not understand and then deliver insult upon insult to the investment professionals. Increasingly I now hear the complaint, 'This used to be a great business to be in but it just isn't anymore.'

And the costs just build up in the form of higher commissions, management fees and levies, all of them paid by you in the end and all of them draining your investment returns away from you. It does no good to complain to your investment adviser about it. He has ever less time for you. He is too busy filling in the mountain of regulatory paperwork that now lands on his desk.

And there you have social evolution without survival of the fittest. If the regulators needed your permission to work for your interests and had to submit a full annual bill to you for all their own costs and the costs they impose on others, I very much doubt that you would employ them for even another day. I think they instinctively know this. They therefore make you out to be an innocent in a bad, bad world that you do not understand. Then it becomes obvious that you need their protection. Then they don't need to ask you. Then you would not even know enough to know that you need them.

But, to repeat myself a hundredth time, the thing with investment is that you have to take charge of your own life. You need to keep your own watch on sharp practice in the market. The law cannot do it for you every time, often cannot do it for you at all and, even more often, cannot compensate you when you are the victim of it. The market may carry out a great deal of its own self-discipline but this does not absolve you of responsibility for your own financial affairs.

What you need from the law is first of all a requirement for full and prompt disclosure, by any company in which the public has any investment, of all corporate doings that could have a significant impact on the share price. What you need more than that is an actively enforced law against fraud. Let those disclosures be signed and dated. If they later prove to be deliberate falsehoods then apply the law's normal sanctions against fraud.

I am afraid it will not happen. The regulators will just grow ever more numerous and their rulebooks ever bulkier and more contrived. This is a burden you will just have to carry. I see no way of getting it off your back.

Money laundering

At the end of the eighteenth century the government of Britain faced a dilemma. The regular wars with France had reached an intensity never endured before and the treasury needed new sources of revenue. Where could it turn?

Import taxes, on which the government had long relied, could supply little more money. Smugglers had become adept at bypassing customs officers and support from the ruling classes for this form of taxation was lukewarm anyway. The tax fell most heavily on French wines, brandy and other luxury goods, which hit the pockets of the ruling classes. Taxing land usage was similarly not considered. The ruling classes owned the land.

Thus did the income tax come into being. It fell most heavily on those newcomers to wealth, the urban middle class and a rising class of industrialists. This was the point.

And now across the world we all carry the burden of the British ruling class's choice of convenience. Government authority is defined by geographical borders, which makes taxation based on the land within those borders not only the most obvious choice of all forms of tax but the easiest and least costly to collect. Municipal governments already find it so. Vast armies of lawyers and accountants could be directed to more useful work than tax avoidance if national governments had also made this choice.

But they have not. The bedrock of tax systems everywhere are taxes on income and profit, a source that massive international trade and investment flows, aided by modern communications technology, has made elusive to the taxman. Governments had no idea 200 years ago that national borders could become quite so porous. They now have no idea of how to deal with it other than hope that signing multilateral deals with other governments to sniff out the trail of money going across borders will restore their lost taxation authority.

Remember this when you hear government officials talk of stopping money laundering. They like to cite dealing in the proceeds of drug trafficking and they also invariably add the words 'and terrorist financing'. There is little evidence, however, that drug trafficking is much deterred by their efforts against money laundering. There is no evidence at all that terrorist financing is deterred. Terrorists need little financing and what they need is either supplied by conniving regimes or primitive arrangements that never touch the world's banking systems.

The real focus, despite all the talk of terrorism and drug trafficking, is rather tax evasion. Money laughs at borders. Companies operating across the world have little difficulty finding where best to book their profits to keep their taxes down.

But government efforts against money laundering have in recent years given individuals more problems, particularly if they invest internationally and maintain bank accounts in different countries. Then their banks ask them every few months for ever more details about where they got their money and what other accounts they hold. It amounts to an unending drip, drip, drip of insinuations of criminality. Private bankers must now write essays for their compliance departments about the extent of the relationship with every individual for whom they act.

I once jokingly suggested to a private banker of my acquaintance that we go into business together to concoct client stories for dubious clients, complete with bogus documentation, at half a million dollars a pop. His nervous laughter told me this was not a new concept to him, and that my suggested price might be in the market range for some clients.

Even doing it honestly is a huge annoyance and also an expensive one, with all the costs landing on your shoulders in the end through brokers' and investment managers' commissions and fees.

I have only one piece of advice for you about this – Give in to it. Fill in every piece of paper they give to you, tick the 'No' box for everything, tell them you understand it all (an improbability) then sign it and send it back well within the deadlines you are given. You have no alternative now. It is either this or the mattress for your savings. Your bank and investment accounts will be frozen or closed if you refuse.

It is all just pro forma, however, and the processors are so overwhelmed by this tsunami of paper that as long as the tick boxes are filled and the signature dated, it is filed and forgotten. It is a tsunami because the more assertive the campaign against money laundering, the more stridently that lower-level bank staff are lectured on the bank's Know-Your-Client rules and the more reports they must file on every 'suspicious transaction' that crosses their desks, just to protect their jobs. Go with the flow and do not make your name stand out for non-compliance with their demands.

Above all, never close a bank account of your own volition. It may be impossible to open again.

CHAPTER 5

The Asian markets

Freedom of speech is not a right that an investment analyst is wise to indulge. Trouble awaits even the mildest criticism if the dealing room is minded the other way. Sometimes 'Sell' is a four-letter word that you must no more than whisper into ears on the desk. Even then you must be prepared for the instant retort of, 'What! You had better be sure of yourself!' It is one reason that investment reports are so often banal and inconclusive.

Things are not so bad in journalism, but even in the newsroom one does best to be polite when fingers meet keyboard. The editor particularly hates to hear the word 'defamatory' and winces just as you would at the third complaining phone call of the day. I confess to having been the cause of it on occasion – I have always considered a bout of Singapore-bashing to be a fine manly sport for a Hong Kong newspaper and I have not always been able to restrain this weakness.

'Did you really *have* to?' says the editor in exasperation. But this is the worst I ever heard from him/her on the subject. An economist of my acquaintance, however, lost his job with a big American investment bank for having done it and his was really more Singapore tickle than Singapore bash.

The fetters are off now. I am retired. Thus here follows the sort of review of Asian investment opportunities which you might expect from a liberated commentator.

But first a general preface. When international investors talk of 'emerging markets' they tend to lump them all together across the world. Thailand, Bolivia and Turkey are treated as one.

Not so quick, say I. Let others comment on the relative merits of Bolivia and Turkey but Asian markets have strengths that others do not have, particularly in equality of opportunity and limits to excesses of corporate power. I cannot always put my finger on how this holds true and I admit that I can put my finger on many examples, as you can, of where it has not done so. Nonetheless I think it is generally true and I attribute it mostly to the influence of Buddhism, which, I believe, has created a background of tolerance and mutual respect not apparent to the same degree elsewhere. I think it a very strong underpinning for financial markets and a reason that people do not speak of European tigers or South American tigers as they do of Asian tigers.

Take note also that in offering my views on individual markets in Asia I am not telling you where to put your money now with follow-up recommendations in a few weeks' time. These are longer-term perspectives. We shall go country by country roughly west to east, finishing with the biggest of them all.

Pakistan

Let me get it off my chest right away. The Pakistani financier with whom the London-based bank for which I was working at the time was most associated was a man named Salman Taseer. I esteemed him hugely, a brilliant and considerate human who served in senior positions in several Pakistani governments. He was then murdered by a religious fanatic for upholding the cause of a Christian woman condemned to death for having reportedly insulted the prophet Muhammad. It colours my thinking of Pakistan. There, I have it off my chest.

There may be some hope for this place in the future if it ever comes to a settlement with India on the sovereignty of Kashmir but until then it will be what it has been since its founding, crushed by an oversize military budget and military dominance of the economy. Making things worse for Pakistan is its growing religious fanaticism, which is not entirely its own fault but certainly does investment prospects no good. I made good friends there and was always received warmly but I have to say that unless this Kashmir business is resolved, and the military burden reduced, there are better places to explore for investment.

India

A land of civil servants, made for civil servants and run by civil servants for the benefit of civil servants. The late Milton Friedman attributed it to India having gained independence from Britain at a time when the fashionable British political philosophy of the day was something called Fabian socialism. I am not so sure. British bureaucracy in India long predated Fabian socialism and I think Indian bureaucrats could always give as well as they received in the fine art of social control.

The firm I was with opened an office in Mumbai shortly after the big economic reform in 1991, the abolition of the commercial licensing requirement. The market did very well then for a period. This, however, was the last big reform. There have been none since then, certainly not of the shake-it-loose-and-let-it-run-free kind. The civil service culture survived that last shake and won't have one again.

Funny thing this, when you consider that ethnic Indians make up a disproportionate number of economists and investment commentators around the world. They really do. And the notable thing about these pundits when they stand up at an investment seminar to present their thoughts, usually well considered, is that they routinely conclude, 'And we therefore think that high among the markets in which you should take an overweight position is . . . India.'

Well, maybe they do not always pick their own ancestral homeland but I cannot remember the last time that one did not.

My advice is to stay underweight. Yes, I know I have devoted a whole book so far to saying that everything knowable to the price of a security is already in the price of that security and it is as true for India as anywhere. Thus the price should be right for what the stock is now. But I still say that India is going nowhere fast. That civil service burden is just too heavy. There are some Indian investments that manage to squeeze out from under the weight of the bureaucrats and, if you find one, you may have a treasure. Yet I doubt you will ever find enough to have a relative overweight position in India.

And one more thing. Why does India have to be so filthy? The dirt and the rubbish really get to you sometimes when you are there. Other countries in as poor a condition have cleaned up much more. It should not be an investment criterion but it does make doing any research there less pleasant.

Sri Lanka
An example of a country that is easily as poor as India but has cleaned up a good deal more. However, there is still not much here for portfolio investment. Sri Lanka's time will come. You have time.

Bangladesh
Never went. My business was stocks, not T-shirts.

Myanmar
Somewhere over the rainbow. . . .

Laos
Ditto but further on the other side of the rainbow.

Cambodia
Ditto, but perhaps nearer by on this side of the rainbow.

Thailand
I sometimes think the centre of Bangkok should feature an oversize dashboard clock marked RPM – Revolutions Per Month. Just when is the military not planning a coup, staging one or promising to return to the barracks from one? It's the national sport and it dominates news about Thailand abroad.

Yet Thailand is also one of the better examples of my dictum that markets disregard politics unless it directly affects their operations, which in Thailand it rarely does. Underneath all the flim-flam of who is boss in Bangkok, the police direct the traffic just as they did before, the government servants come in to work on time, the trains run, the planes fly, the kids go to school, the street stalls serve street food, life is normal. On the market some people take fright and sell but the bargain hunters soon come along and all plods quietly along again.

I think a big reason for this stability is that Thailand is one of the very few countries of Asia to have resisted European colonisation. Its civil service has always been homegrown, its industries risen from local roots and its economy adapted to the needs of Thailand. Unbroken independence brings a strong continuity of administration.

This is not to say that all has been a steady advance for Thai financial markets. The 1990s were a decade of loose monetary controls in a vain attempt to make Bangkok an international financial centre. There was an accompanying real-estate bubble and a big boom on the stock market. I remember telling one client at the time that a big new listing in which he wanted some shares was a sheaf of architect's blueprints valued at two per cent of Thailand's gross domestic product. He thought I overstated the case, which I may have done, but never by as much as the listing price overstated the stock's underlying value. It was not the only stock to have lost touch with reality.

Then along came a big crash in the 1998 Asian financial crisis. It hurt and I am glad to say that Thailand has since learned lessons from that chapter of its history. We have since been back to steady-as-you-go Thailand. It all moves to the background drumbeat of the usual military coups but with a sensible, competent bureaucracy, capable industrialists, a soundly grounded economy and thriving financial markets. Thailand is one of my choices for an overweight investment position in Asia.

Vietnam

To many people of my generation Vietnam is a name of grim connotations. If emigration from the Netherlands had taken my family a few miles south of the Canadian border instead of north of it, I would been eligible for the US Army draft and very likely sent to Vietnam. I know some people who had been and I can't say the experience did any of them good. I had draft dodgers as dorm neighbours at university in Vancouver and despite being a non-combatant, Canada's campuses were the scene of constant anti-war demonstrations.

Which is why my first visit to Vietnam years later left me puzzled. How could there be so little sign of this war? In Hanoi the focus of the war museum is the 1950s liberation war with the French while in Saigon the roof of the old presidential palace features a mouldering helicopter from the 1960s and the basement a line of old teletype machines from the same era. That's about it and there are not many people about. North of Da Nang I saw some bomb craters at an archaeological site and, when I pointed them out to our guide, he said only, 'They missed.' What was there to hit? You feel uneasy about raising the subject with the Vietnamese, however, and they don't volunteer. If the talk comes up it is usually soon diverted.

How can so many people live through so prolonged and horrible an experience and show so little effect from it? In North Korea, for instance, where the suffering from an earlier war was worse, I am convinced it plays a part in the persistent hermit nature of the regime. You cannot really expect these people, even decades afterward, to turn around and say, 'Well, maybe we got our economic policy wrong. Maybe we should do it the way it's done where the people came from who killed my family.' Not going to happen, not for three or four generations anyway.

It is why I think that Vietnam, after North Korea, still remains perhaps the most doctrinaire of the old-line communist regimes of Asia. They may hide it but I think a lot of that pain still lies at the back of their heads. They will not quickly change who they are and how they live when they fought so hard for it back then.

Superficially, in any case, there is not much to tell them they should change. The economy, always well supported by its lush agricultural base, is now also booming with the spillover of China's manufacturing industries. Vietnam is becoming an Asian tiger.

And yet, and yet ... it is still almost all low-wage, low-return assembly work with little movement upmarket and not much in the way of a market ladder to move up anyway. A few people make the money while millions more grind their lives away with mind-numbing labour in the cause of keeping Western consumers happy. It may be an industrious society but I would not call it an entrepreneurial one. Command economies are like that.

And then there is that other import from China, pervasive corruption. I have heard stories of it on all sides, enough to make me rate the Vietnam public sector as one of the most corrupt in Asia although, I grant you, this is hearsay. They do not pick directly on foreigners much. Not too long ago, for instance, I was on a cruise downriver from Hanoi, watching a police boat speed up to the sand barge ahead of us, make a brief contact and then turn to our vessel before swerving away on sight of me.

'They're collecting, probably for the local police chief's daughter's wedding or something like that,' I was told. 'They won't hit us with you standing there.' They certainly hit everyone else.

I admit that the Singapore hedge fund of which I was a director blunted itself on Vietnamese investments. The picks were good, but the Vietnamese dong was always a sad currency and our local staff saw little point in employer loyalty while there was an active job market for English speakers. There are a few headhunters whose necks I could cheerfully wring. Perhaps it influences my thinking but here is that thinking anyway: For personal portfolio investment Vietnam's time is probably still a little further in the future.

Malaysia

How strange that I should speak of pervasive corruption in Vietnam and not make the comparison to Malaysia where it is more occasional but then much greater. When people connected to the government of the day in Kuala Lumpur stick their hands in the till they are not looking for coins. It got so bad at one point that the country called a ninety-three-year-old ex-prime minister back to office because he was the only honest one they could find when the sitting one was linked to a multi-billion-dollar pocket lining. It did not really surprise me. Most serious financial scandals in Hong Kong in the 1980s had a Malaysian angle.

Two immediate reasons for it stand out. The first is royalty. Every one of the Malaysian states has a sultan or chief minister of almost equal status. These people and their extended families believe themselves entitled to the good things of life. This means that if they don't have what they think they should have they often just grab it. It is a contagious state of mind. It infects the entire government.

The second is the division of races. Ethnic Chinese account for about a quarter of the population and they dominate the business life of the country. The Malays control the government, the army and the slice of the financial sector they can appropriate to themselves by law. It was never enough to maintain equality of income between the two races, however, and post-colonial history has featured outbursts of racial unrest. At one point Chinese businesses were forced to divest 30 per cent of their ownership to Malay businesses and institutions.

It did not work as well as expected. The bigger of these businesses were listed on the stock markets of both Kuala Lumpur and Singapore. A Hong Kong stockbroking company for which I was working at the time also had a Singapore representative office. We made a lot of money that year taking big chunks of these 30 per cent shareholdings from the new Malay owners at a discount and selling them back to the original Chinese owners out of sight of Kuala Lumpur. The Malaysian authorities complained to Singapore about it eventually and our representative office licence proved unrenewable. I cannot deny complicity. I was not directly involved but some of my bonus that year came from it.

I have to say that I think Malaysia has had its day. Its economy boomed in colonial days with tin and rubber and in post-colonial days with palm oil. But tin was the wonder metal of the nineteenth century, not the present one, while condoms and surgical gloves do not quite make up for car tyres now that synthetics have largely replaced natural rubber on the road. As to those vast plantations of oil palm, almost every country in the tropics grows tree grease these days and it is not a particularly healthy food oil in the hydrogenated form in which it is sold. It is certainly not the big new winner it was fifty years ago.

What is left?

A decent bit, actually. The transport and other infra-structure is very good. This was always a positive feature of British colonial history. British engineers revelled in the possibilities of Asia and they built well. It has been kept up. The financial infrastructure is also soundly based. Chinese banks tend to be glorified pawn shops (it is the way across Asia) and Malay financial institutions have found from painful experience that it is a good model to follow. In public life Malaysia is a functioning democracy, rule of law is upheld and the courts do not model themselves on royalty in matters of payment.

It's just that where the future is concerned Malaysia is one of those places where I think it really is already in the price. I can see it doing well but I cannot see it finding some new unrecognised potential. In investment terms this is the more settled Asia, not the new Asia. That would still make it a congenial framework for investment except that it always stands to be undermined by corruption and race tension. There will be reason from time to time to have an overweight investment presence in Malaysia but these times will be intermittent.

Singapore

The country closest in the world to having achieved communism in the classic Marxist sense of the word would hardly seem a fit candidate for a regular ranking as the world's freest economy after Hong Kong. Yet it is an accolade that American think tanks regularly award Singapore. I can only recommend to these supposed thinkers that they get out of the tank occasionally and pay Singapore (and Hong Kong) a visit.

In Singapore what is not directly owned or controlled by the bureaucrats is still directly under their thumb. They tell one bank 'Open' and it opens and another bank 'Close' and it closes. There is no crime involved, no financial failures, only a shift of government policy, and a mouse can squeak louder than the protest to be heard from the losers of such shifts. The Boss rules.

In one way I can understand that' freest economy' tag. It is easy to confuse a free economy with a parasite economy and Singapore vies with Hong Kong for the distinction of being the most notable parasite economy of Asia. Singapore's role is to do for its neighbours, primarily Malaysia and Indonesia, what they themselves cannot do or, for reasons of state or perceived morality, will not do. Finance obviously figures high in this and officialdom knows not to ask too many questions. I remember once recommending an over-weight position in Indonesia to a group of Singapore bankers, only to be met by a rolling of eyes, which said as loudly as words, 'Look, you idiot, where do you think we get our money?'

Things to do for others have also traditionally included such services as a port, ship repair, a big air travel way stop and fancy shopping. Whoever labelled the British a nation of shopkeepers, for instance, had certainly never been to Singapore.

But Indonesia and Malaysia are catching up in these sectors of the economy and Singapore cannot count on holding its edge forever. This has long been recognised by the bureaucrats and the choice they made at the time for a bedrock industry was high-tech manufacturing.

I hear you. How does a wealthy, tiny island country with a minuscule domestic market, no tradition of manufacturing skill sets or innovation and no significant intellectual property rights make itself a manufacturing powerhouse in fancy digital equipment?

Simple. You go to the big foreign names in such things and offer them cheap land, low taxes, financial assistance, an imported labour force from as far away as China, everything they could want if only they come to Singapore.

And they did come. The manufacturing contribution to gross domestic product rose to 25 per cent.

What came, however, was mostly the low end of high tech, the click-the-bits-together-and-put-them-in-a-box end. It also primed no pumps and reached no critical mass among Singaporeans themselves. Manufacturing investment commitments remained 90 per cent foreign. This is a society of administrators, not entrepreneurs. The result is that almost all the winnings of this foreign investment just flow back to the foreign owners. Bear it in mind when Singaporeans boast (their biggest export) of their high GDP per capita. Their disposable income per capita is a good deal less.

I think that, instead of diversifying further out of finance, the Singaporean economy will find itself concentrating more on finance. The future certainly does not lie in manufacturing unless it is one of wilful poverty. Meanwhile the ships and shops face growing competition and an airport does not a country make. I also cannot see Singapore as Hollywood East, a leader of Asian cultural expression, just cannot see it. I can, however, see Singapore as a superb home for the United Nations when the UN finally recognises that New York is the wrong one.

But what is so bad about relying on banking and investment? Singapore does this well. My own personal portfolio has a hefty weighting of a Singapore pawn shop nicknamed Only Can Borrow Coin, plus a line of debt-market instruments arranged and registered in Singapore and thus under the protection of Singapore law. It is good law. Unless you are in court because you have embarrassed the government you are in safe hands with Singapore judges.

It does not take much to be overweight (foodwise, too) in so small a market as Singapore. You may easily find yourself so. It still will not amount to much in your portfolio.

Indonesia

No-one these days has much good, or much of anything, to say about President Suharto who ruled over Indonesia for thirty-one years. Let me speak for him anyway. Indonesia is not a country. Indonesia is an empire, the Javanese Empire governed from Jakarta on the island of Java and comprising a wide range of ethnicities, religions and wealth disparity over its countless islands. An empire is not easy to administer and Suharto did it the classical imperial way. Let any group get seriously out of line and the Emperor would send a messenger – 'Daddy doesn't like this. Better not do it again.' If done again, the messenger would also call again – 'Daddy is very unhappy about this. Do it again and you will make him angry.' If done a third time the army/police would take the messenger's place and their response could be heavy and violent.

It worked. The tensions that strain Indonesia were restrained during Suharto's rule. It still works today despite an occasional spectacle of community or religious outrage. The Roman Empire certainly never enjoyed such a state of relative peace.

I think it is at last bringing Indonesia to a state of more robust industrial growth. The lessons of past monetary indiscipline have been learned and the drag of constant fiscal and current-account deficits recognised. The physical infrastructure is also slowly growing better although visitors would do well not to take the airport at which they land as a statement of the entire country. This is a rule across Asia, by the way. Everyone is building fancy airports. Go a few miles further out before you really start to look.

I would not quite call it take-off time for Indonesia yet. These things go slowly across an empire of 260 million people. Yet, given the modern trends of technology transfer, low shipping costs, rapid communications and foreign investment, this is a quarter billion people eager to follow where China has led. They will work for less pay than is now the China standard and politicians in America and Europe do not fear Indonesia as they do China.

Yes, I know many people still have marks against Indonesia for Javanese territorial ambition, corruption, overbearing bureaucracy and Muslim militancy. I cannot entirely refute these criticisms. On the other side of this coin I have often found myself delighting in the remarkable inventiveness and initiative of these people. Indonesia is one of my confident overweight choices.

Papua New Guinea
Somewhere over the rainbow? What rainbow? Don't see no rainbow.

Australia

I once overheard my office assistant giving trouble to a junior for her grouping of countries on a mailing list.

'You've got it all wrong, you dunce,' she said. 'You put Australia in with Europe. Australia doesn't belong with Europe. Australia belongs with North America.'

Spot on, an insight of genius. Canada has its British Columbia and Australia has its British California. What more apt description could there be of New South Wales? You can certainly count on the fingers of one hand how many people in Asia think Australia lies in their part of the world.

Philippines

Another country with strong links to America. Think of the Philippines as a piece of Latin America which floated across the Pacific Ocean 500 years ago and you have a worthwhile insight on the place. It has not all been a happy history. First the Spanish were brutal to the native population and then the Americans were even more brutal with a culminating destruction of Manila at the cost of more than 100,000 Philippine lives in 1945.

The outcome, mysteriously, is still the cheeriest people on Earth. There is laughter and music wherever you go in the Philippines. Try this test some time. Ask your taxi driver on the way from the airport in Manila to turn on the radio and surf the channels. Every one of them will be a music channel. Do it in Hong Kong and what you will get is a recitation of numbers – race results, stock market closings, temperature forecasts, winning lottery numbers, etc.

But I have to say that the Philippines is also one of the world's goofier countries. I can think of no better word for it. Where else, when a military conspiracy has a presidential candidate shot at the bottom of the aircraft stairs on his return from exile, would the commemorative statue have him standing right by an exact copy of those airstairs with a dove perched on his shoulder on the side from which the shot came? Bizarre. You will find it in the Makati Triangle. That's the Philippines, musical, laughter-filled, violent and, I'm afraid there is only one word for it, goofy.

They have also yet to get over the colonial legacy that has long kept them in poverty. The volcanic island of Negros, for instance, is little but sugar plantation from the sea all the way up the mountain, interspersed by sugar mills and military outposts. The mills pay the sugar croppers in warehouse receipts for the estimated sugar content of their cane, little bits of paper that can only be sold to discounters in the squalid little villages that line the main roadway and are all called 'city'. The military outposts here and there among the cane fields ensure that the poverty does not translate into active membership of the communist New People's Army. It is a vision from the eighteenth century. Why can the Philippines still not emerge from it? Why is there still such a wealth gap of Latin American proportions? I have no answer.

And then you have the millions of Philippine overseas contract workers, mostly women who entrust their own children to relatives and go abroad so that they can help raise the children of foreigners and wash the backsides of patients at geriatric hospitals. Their remittances, badly needed at home, constitute a significant part of the Philippine gross domestic product. They are still cheery on their days off, you just cannot wring it out of the Philippine character, but something has failed in any economic system that forces many of its people to leave their families for years.

And yet, and yet, I think the Philippines is slowly growing out of it. I concede that my more positive outlook on the investment picture might have something to do with a Philippine stock being the all-time best performer of my personal portfolio but, then again, this is not a bad indicator. My view is that there is still a great deal of opportunity to be realised here. Even if it is a slow realisation of that opportunity with regular setbacks along the way, I think it a sure one. The Philippines is another of my confident overweight recommendations.

Hong Kong

A parasite economy like Singapore, Hong Kong has always thrived by doing for mainland China what China cannot itself do, or, for reasons of public policy, will not do, and by adapting quickly when change comes to China. Over Hong Kong's history this has meant a transition from drug trafficking to shipping to garment manufacturing and, most recently, to services, principally financial services and, high among them, money laundering.

Tut, tut, tut, not supposed to say that. All I can demonstrate is that three times over ten years Hong Kong's annual capital inflows exceeded 100 per cent of gross domestic product and, curiously, were exactly matched by capital outflows of the same size. Now, just how might that happen in full accordance with the law? Hmmm . . . let us look the other way.

But the big question is what Hong Kong can do next. The port is in slow decline with new ports in the Mainland being more obvious and less costly shipment centres. Export manufacturing has vanished and high-tech ambitions have all proved a means of flushing away money, as have dreams of making the city an education centre and a medical centre. Government officials obsess themselves with the question every day. I doubt, however, that they will find the answer. Hong Kong has always made its big economic transitions without, or against, their guidance, which is invariably just to keep pouring more resources into yesterday's ideas.

As in Singapore, I think financial services will still be an excellent support to the economy for years to come. The big strength, as in Singapore, is rule of law, which everyone trusts (with the exception in Hong Kong of the times that it would embarrass the big boss in Beijing). There are also free financial markets from which government generally keeps itself distant and a long history in the many facets of financial services. The putative competition across the border talks big of having all this as well but the boss is always superior to the law in China and capital allocation is state controlled. I see no immediate threat to Hong Kong's standing from this direction.

The real threat lies elsewhere. Few people doubt Beijing's right to sovereignty as it is cold, hard fact that Britain stole Hong Kong from China by armed robbery for the purpose of drug trafficking in the mid-nineteenth century. This historical wrong has now been righted. It is also perfectly obvious to anyone who thinks about it that Hong Kong could not survive on its own if it was cut off from China. Parasites cannot live without their hosts.

Yet hosts must also respect the autonomy of their parasites for a thriving symbiotic relationship and, while China has pledged Hong Kong's autonomy, it has become steadily more obvious that the direction of affairs is in the hands of secretive Beijing-appointed officials who make all their decisions behind closed doors. The purpose of these puppeteers is China's greater glory as envisioned by the ruling party and Hong Kong's subjugation to this vision, willing if it can be had, forced if not.

The result has been a timid government of unelected civil servants who squander Hong Kong's resources for the support of key business constituencies. In financial markets it is notable by a relaxation of standards and a too-ready acceptance of dubious Mainland listings on the stock market. All of this slowly grinds away at Hong Kong's core strengths. It has been made apparent by repeated instances of civil unrest, the most serious of them following a government attempt in 2019 to introduce a much-feared extradition bill.

I have made Hong Kong my home. It is a magical city in a thousand different ways but in one of them I do not like the magic as much as I once did. My longer-term advice is to be generally underweight in this market.

Taiwan

I am not a great believer in high-tech, at least not for personal investment. Labelling an industry 'high-tech' does a wonderful job of impressing politicians but most of the work is actually low-tech assembly in high-tech surroundings and all too often the intellectual property rights, if any, are only worth much for a few months before they are supplanted by something else. Give me high-tech for my living room or the den, please, but give me low-tech for my portfolio.

Taiwan has long been a leader in high-tech across Asia and some of its industry leaders have undoubtedly done very well, the big wafer fab TSMC for instance. But Taiwan is also an island of only 24 million people and it has a hard time keeping all that it has started. Apple Inc.'s biggest supplier, for instance, a Taiwan start-up, simply outgrew Taiwan and was forced to develop its biggest production facilities in China. And then there is that oh-so-deep respect for intellectual property rights, which so characterises entrepreneurial activity in China. Let those pirates catch a glimpse of what you are doing and it is gone.

If Taiwan's high-tech talent did not have China next door it might easily have outshone Silicon Valley. But Taiwan is where it is and can do nothing about it. China treats the island as a rebel province that will soon be re-absorbed and the people must live under this threat every day. This has bred a national character that is clearly distinct from China's and growing more so steadily. Yet there is no getting away from that looming presence across the straits. China is where the running is at present and China is not minded to do Taiwan any favours.

You have to be cold-hearted about these things when you invest. It is a drag on the performance of Taiwanese financial markets. Scout the place for opportunity by all means but I doubt that you will consistently find yourself with a heavy weighting there.

South Korea

A country obsessed with proving itself to the world. It should not be surprising, really, if you consider that when bigger neighbours on all sides, principally Japan, looked at Korea over the centuries, they smacked their lips and said, 'That will do nicely for a colony.'

The Koreans are now out to show them how nicely a former colony can do for itself. Move aside, Sony, here comes Samsung. On your knees, Honda, Hyundai is upon you. And it is not only Japan they want to show. They have a love/hate relationship with the US, too, because of the Korean War, in fact, a whole world they wish to tell about the Korean miracle. Here comes the K-Pop to assault your ears.

For insights into Korean obsessions you may note that for many years South Korea has had the highest suicide rate of the developed world, that it has a greater failing than even America's Bible Belt for quasi-Protestant evangelical movements and that prison is a very common retirement destination for Korean presidents. It is an odd phenomenon on the streets of Seoul that many young women look alike. They have all gone to the same plastic surgery clinic for the same chin job.

But then how easy is it for these people to live normal lives when thousands of North Korean heavy artillery pieces just to the north across the border are sighted permanently on their heads? There are reasons for the obsessions that mark them.

My personal frustration is that they would tell me so little about them on my visits. The company guide takes you to the product display room and leaves you there. Well, if you are not a customer who cares about you? When you visit a think tank (lots of them about) you are shown to the tiny office of the man who speaks to foreigners and he, opening the statistics book of which he has let you hold a copy, says, 'Regarding the economic growth rate of the Republic of South Korea, you will see on the sixth line from the bottom of page 13, one, two, three, four, no, pardon me, the fifth line from the bottom, that the economic growth rate of the Republic of South Korea in the second quarter of this calendar year was 5.67 per cent greater on a year over year annualised basis than in the second quarter of the previous year on a year over year annualised basis and, as you will see on page 14, line seven, yes, no, yes, line seven, we have forecast an equivalent forecast figure for the third quarter of this calendar year of 5.76 per cent.' He then closes his book, next question, please.

What have you learned from such a visit?

In my view you have learned that when Koreans develop an obsession with proving themselves they will pull out all the stops to do it. You may then be permitted to participate in the fruits of this effort provided you do not bother yourself too much with finding a direct chain of cause and effect between intent and achievement. I think it still holds true. Korea is one of my picks for renewed growth.

Japan

Here is a joke for you from the 1980s. President Ronald Reagan falls asleep, Rip Van Winkle style, for a number of years, and becomes agitated when he wakes up. 'What's happened to the United States while I nodded off?' he asks his aides. 'Don't worry about it, Mr President,' they reply. 'Everything's fine. The economy's booming, the deficit is gone and inflation is down to zero. If you don't believe it, just go down the street to McDonald's. A Big Mac will still cost you only two hundred yen.'

Hah, hah, hah, you will say (I hope) if you are over forty. If you are under forty you will say, 'I don't get it.'

What there is to get is the American experience of the Japan that could say 'No', the Japan of the 1980s that had resurged from the ruins of the Pacific War to overwhelm the world with the unbeatable standard of its industrial products and the fabled 'Japanese Way'. For price, build quality, reliability and technical sophistication no American car maker could come close to the Japanese competition while American consumer electronics producers simply vanished. 'Takes a licking and keeps on ticking', said the ad for Timex watches. Seiko and Casio gave Timex a licking and the ticking was the count on the first-round knockout. The Japanese industrial victory right along the aisles of every shopping mall was stunning. It could have been their way of saying 'Take that for Hiroshima' but they didn't say it. They just took their winnings and proceeded to buy up prize American real estate, renowned movie studios and the US national debt. An international summit was President Reagan, Japanese Prime Minister Yasuhiro Nakasone and perhaps a West German chancellor, perhaps not. It naturally frightened Americans. The US dollar might be the next to go. How much does a Big Mac cost in yen?

But where is that Japan now?

Gone, symbolised in a soft-mannered old Emperor who shuffled around on his cane, a metaphor for the entire country. They still make good consumer tat but rarely at the leading edge any longer. They now have one of the world's oldest populations and that fierce drive is no longer in evidence. Japan has stalled and others have gone past it.

I think it mostly has to do with malinvestment, with government debt at more than 200 per cent of gross domestic product after a long line of failed stimulus attempts. One administration after another thrashes about, blindly groping for the secret of renewed growth and every one of them just makes this malady of weariness worse. Something like it also affects the Japanese corporate world.

I have held a position in the Japanese stock market for a number of years and what the stocks have given me the yen has largely taken away. I could have done better elsewhere. Perhaps it's time to put that thought into action. In investment terms Japan is yesterday's story. I doubt that you will carry a heavy weighting there.

China

I think myself a fair man. If I hold certain opinions that can be tested to see if they are correct, then bring on that test and let it run without anyone tinkering with it. In fact, if people who take the opposing view from mine on where China is headed wish to tinker with the test to influence it their way, please, go ahead. Stack the test against me. Do it even more. Like Elijah with the priests of Baalim, bring it on. I am still confident of what it will show.

My confidence is rooted in the power of the marketplace to discover in that unimaginably convoluted and dynamic thing called the economy just what will serve the most people the best at the lowest price they need pay. I am a great believer in natural selection. I am a product of it. So are you.

Others look at this matter differently. What I call the marketplace they call capitalism and they see it as dominated by overweight old white men greedily wringing even the indigent dry of the last resources that keep them alive. Why allow this to happen, they ask, when we, the people, can take charge of our affairs to redistribute the wealth from everyone according to his ability to everyone according to his need? Let us do it and when it is done we may eventually be able to abolish even government to achieve the true natural state of human society.

Now I may say that it is actually such tinkering with the natural function of an economy that creates wealth disparity. I can say that a marketplace left to its own devices will, of its own workings, take the great wealth of any one individual and spread it widely again over two or three generations. It cannot be done overnight, I admit, not as fast as it can be taken from that individual by force in a command economy, but it is nonetheless more certain. I can say all of this but why bother when in the world of real events we can have an actual demonstration, a real full test of whether a command economy can do what it claims to do? This test is being played out in China right now.

You may hear that, uniquely in the world, China has a combination economy of 'Chinese characteristics', a command and market economy combined. I think the notion essentially racist. We are talking of how human enterprise and human resources interact. There is no special species of human in China to make this process fundamentally different from how it operates in the rest of the world. If you combine a command economy with a market economy what you get is a corrupt command economy. A command economy does not brook challenge to its essential powers. Control of how the money is raised and where it is allocated must rest in the hands of the bosses. Let a market economy truly operate unhindered beneath this and all the money will go to that market. That will then be the end of the command economy. Thus while some toying has been allowed with the forms of a market in China the allocation and pricing of capital remains firmly in the hands of the bosses.

I say that China's economic growth is increasingly a delusion. It is powered by taking money from the people through their bank deposits and sending it to the state's chosen industries and projects. The measure of worthwhile capital expenditure, always and everywhere, is return on investment, but when it is ignored the result is that ever more money is wasted on overcapacity in industries that have no restraints on investment.

Steel production at seven or more times what Europe turns out is needed to build the ships, ports, railways, highways and bridges by which the iron ore from Australia goes to the steel mills so that these can supply more steel to build the ships, ports, railways, etc., to bring the iron ore from Australia. . . . Round and round again this industry chases its tail.

But what is produced must be used. Overcapacity in cement has led to construction of vast but empty housing estates. They may have been sold but mostly to speculators whose bets must be supported by price supports or the balloon will start to deflate and then there may be no stopping it.

None of this is to gainsay the remarkable improvement in the living standards of the Chinese people over the last forty years. Equally, this was not so much the outcome of economic policies adopted in Beijing as of enormous worldwide improvements over the same period in technology transfer, access to international finance, rapid communications, digital-control technology and swiftly falling shipping costs. The challenge to Beijing was whether it would allow China to conform itself to these trends. It did and it reaped the rewards. Nonetheless, there is more to the harvest than the harvesters.

Helping it along at the time that reform from Maoist maladministration finally came to an impoverished China, the wealth across the world of ethnic Chinese expatriate populations was by some measures not much less than that of China itself. A great deal of this money was then readily made available to help the motherland's reforms. The Soviet Union never had such help when it was finally forced to confront its inefficiencies.

Retarding this process was the continuing problem that to pick industrial winners, particularly in manufacturing, you must know what generates the best return on investment, which is not possible to do in a system that selects investment by government policy rather than by return. You get losers that way, not winners. It can, however, be done if instead of funding it in yuan you use US dollars sourced in an open market, which is what China's export manufacturing mostly does. Even the trade figures are reported in US dollars with the yuan equivalents stated as an afterthought.

But then you also encourage all the most profitable work to be done abroad. For example, in making a clock there are many steps between concept and final delivery into the customer's hands. Where China has figured is in forming the housings, assembling the parts and stamping 'Made In China' on the final product. These are the low-margin elements and it is hard to rise above them when you do not know if you can access yuan financing at rates that really reflect open market demand or when you cannot get any finance at all because it has been allocated elsewhere on policy grounds.

Also keeping so much of the economy at the low end of production is suppression of wages through a pernicious system that denies workers social and legal rights unless they are resident in their district of registry. They are mostly not so in the big production centres. The cost push upwards from the bottom is therefore restrained.

How long can this continue before the weight of all the inefficiencies becomes too much to carry? Good question and if I could answer it I would not have written a book saying that no-one is clever enough to have the precise answer to such questions. I am sure, however, that the state-sponsored assault on sound credit has already significantly weakened what passes for a banking system. This is crucial because, as repositories of the people's wealth, these banks are proportionately twice as important as are their American counterparts.

But I don't think it will end with a burst balloon as in the spectacular collapse of the Soviet Union. I think it will end the Asian way, no big bang, just a long whimper. Slowly the whole system will grow tired under the weight of a continued misallocation of capital and an ageing population, just as it did in Japan. This might even be considered a reasonable and less catastrophic way of correcting the inefficiencies than a Soviet-style crash. There are people who say it is so in Japan. But then the correction will take a long, long time to come fully through.

This could still leave you with some reasonable prospects in the China stock market, except for one debilitating factor. A healthy financial market requires a proper balance between the interests of investors and of issuers. Swing it all to investor protection and no issuers will come. Swing it all to issuers and investors will get tired of never making any money. The China financial markets swing too much to the second of these two poles. From the perspective of the state the purpose of financial markets is purely to offer an alternative to bank financing and direct state subsidy of industrial investment. The interests of small investors are not considered.

In short, I do not think you will find yourself with a heavy weighting in the China financial markets.

CHAPTER 6

Hot tips

I have none. But here are some general guidelines I think worthwhile.

You are your own best investment adviser. I am all for repetition. It is a good way of fixing a concept firmly in the mind. So here we go again. Investment advisers are experts on *how* and *where* to buy and sell investments but they know nothing more than you do about *what* to buy and *when.* There are no experts in these two crucial questions of investment. The future is obscure to all of us and the present price of every investment already reflects what little can be guessed about its prospects. Look to your own good judgement for the best guidance you can find. To depend on others outright for it is to abdicate your own intelligence. When you have money to invest you face a challenge of intellect. You have to take a view on what the future holds. Anything you do implies such a view. Do not shrink from it. Have some confidence in yourself, take that view with deliberation and make your choices.

As a default strategy, keep your investments in the currency in which you intend eventually to use the money. You cannot always do it, particularly if you live in a small country with its own currency. Sometimes you may have your own good reasons, tax avoidance for instance, not to do it. But in any investment involving a foreign exchange transaction you will find that the gouge on the forex is the biggest of all the middleman's gouges. Bear in mind also Newton's Third Law of Market Motion – To every profitable forex transaction there is an equal and opposite loss reaction. Forex is a zero-sum gain. It generates no wealth of its own, pays no dividends, interest or rent, constitutes no part of food, clothes or shelter. The sum total of all the forex gains and losses across the world every day is zero, less the cost of dealing. If you do not need to expose your portfolio to forex risk and cost, don't.

Pay off your mortgage. This is no absolute guideline. Sometimes it makes more sense to rent than to buy your home. Most people in Germany for instance, are renters. But if you do buy your own home then paying off the mortgage is one of the better investments you can make. Let me buy that mortgage from your bank if you do not believe me. Perhaps I have already done it as I have a substantial holding of mortgage funds. They are a first-class financial asset. My only problem is that the bank through which I hold them takes too big a cut for itself. You can do better than I can, however. You can effectively keep all of that cut for yourself. You can do it by paying off your mortgage as fast as you can and relieving yourself of that cost. The more you pay it down, the more of your monthly mortgage payment goes to paying for that home itself and the less to paying off the bank's interest charges, which just means you pay the mortgage off even faster. Great idea. One of the best.

The only time the whole herd is headed one way is when it is headed to the slaughterhouse. The problem with contrarian investment thinking is that all the people with whom you talk about investment will tell you they are contrarian. Who really wants to say, 'I'm a conventional, boring sort of person. I go with the herd'? Thus it is not always easy to know which way the herd is really headed. But you can know when the herd is *all* headed one way. It is when you find not just your friends, not just your investment adviser, but even you yourself saying things like 'I really can't lose on this one' or 'It's never looked so good as it looks now'. It does not matter that such statements may actually be true for a period. The journey from the feedlot to the slaughterhouse takes a little time. Very few members of the herd, however, stop and walk backwards against the herd on that journey. If you want to be one of those few then tell yourself that you are wrong just when you are happiest that you are right. It is not easy. That is why so few do it. But the slaughterhouse is invariably just over the hill when the whole herd is headed towards that hill.

However wide the exits they are never wide enough for a stampede. It is what algorithm traders most commonly forget. They have programmed their machines for every eventuality that digital brains can conceive but one thing digital brains cannot conceive is that the market may suddenly vanish. Even human brains find it hard to appreciate that suddenly there may be just no bid on the market even if you chase it far, far down. And then even the last bid you have hit is suddenly doubtful because word is sweeping the market that this buyer is no longer good for his money. Get me out, get me out, screams every nerve but the exits are already jammed. There is no getting out. Thus the only thing you can do is stay in. You have no choice anyway and the biggest danger is at the exits. The mood inside is glum but it is not the panic of the exits. And here is the good news. The advent of the bargain hunter is surer than the Second Coming and sooner.

For every adjective you add to the instrument you add two per cent to the fee. Or three or four per cent. Derivatives are a way that investment bankers can keep all the value of their deals while making you take all the risk. You didn't know this, did you? Well, now you do. When you hear talk of puts and calls your best course is to put on your shoes and call for your coat. With ordinary stocks you limit your downside and make your upside infinite while with derivatives you limit your upside and you make your downside infinite. This stuff is not for your personal portfolio. And if it weren't bad enough that derivatives are just a plain bad idea for you, the gouge in dealing costs is a topping of insult. The more complicated the thing is, the more it will cost you in fees and gouges. Just count up those adjectives that define the complications and then multiply by two per cent . . . or three . . . or four.

Onscreen is cheaper than offscreen. This is a variation on that last bit of advice. Liquid investments, those with a reasonable enough level of daily trading to allow you to buy and sell them with relative ease, are generally onscreen. This means that you should be able to find the latest dealt prices or the bid/offers on even the screen of a smartphone with a bit of finger work. If you cannot find them there and must rely on an intermediary's word for where the market in your investment stands then you have an offscreen market. In an offscreen market your dealing costs will be higher and the price quote you get less trustworthy than in an onscreen market.

It's in the price if it's in the press. One of my favourite truths. It should be so very obvious and yet so very many people do not recognise it. As an investment analyst it used to surprise me how many of my colleagues would quote the morning's public newsfeeds as their contribution to market information for the day. This has to be the ultimate example of the dog chasing its own tail. First the analysts tell the journalists what it means and then the journalists tell the analysts and they can cite it as good authority at the next day's morning meeting. By this time the sales desk might as well tell the client that Old McDonald had a farm. Yes, let us have up-to-the-second prices and corporate announcements onscreen everywhere. But the truth is that no-one peddles the obvious quite as consistently as journalists do. Where any insight of value to the *future* movement of the price is concerned, the best state of any digital news device is the state of Off and the best place for any newspaper, financial magazine and newsletter is under the bird cage, where these things have always served the better purpose anyway. The price has seen the future long before the journalists have.

The grass is not greener on the other side. It really is not. The way that market intermediaries make their money is by feeding on you when you start worrying about whether you could have done better in something else. They do it every time you deal and what they take from you is more than they tell you. There is that foreign exchange gouge, for instance, or the fact that you generally buy near the high end of the price range for the day and sell near the low end. Funny that. Remember also that any time you deal you are in the sights of the insider dealers, the front runners and every species of market manipulator. Dealing costs are the single biggest drag on the performance of many personal investment portfolios. Just review the record of all the changes you have either made over a year or for which you kept yourself awake at night by worrying about whether you should make, and then ask yourself how often it was really worthwhile to jump in and out. You will almost certainly agree with me that by far the most times you should just have left that portfolio alone to grow by itself. If in doubt about whether to deal, don't.

> *The market she go up,*
> *The market she go down,*
> *The market she go round and round.*
> *Wanna buy some?*